GW00670204

YORK
City Beautiful

YORK
City Beautiful

Alistair and Jan Campbell

First published in Great Britain in 2009 by
The Breedon Books Publishing Company Limited,
Breedon House, 3 The Parker Centre, Derby,
DE21 4SZ.

A catalogue record for this book is available from the British Library.

ISBN 978-1-85983-691-0

Printed and bound MKT Print, Slovenia

CONTENTS

DEDICATION

In memory of Jan's brother Graham.

'Treasured Memories'

ACKNOWLEDGEMENTS

We would like to acknowledge the contribution and support of the organisations that have so very kindly provided assistance during the writing of this book. Without their extensive co-operation, we would have been unable to create such a varied portfolio of images that portray the City of York.

We would particularly like to thank the following for allowing us the opportunity to capture and authorise the reproduction of images for *York City Beautiful*:

Dean and Chapter of York, York Minster
Jorvik Viking Centre
National Railway Museum, York
The Richard III Museum
The Guildhall and Mansion House, City of York Council
Visit York
York Museums Trust

In addition we would like to note special thanks to:

Jacqui and Karl Cundill, Karen Green, and Muriel and Ken Green.

FOREWORD

Almost every British urban landscape has an aesthetic quality and scene that can entice any visitor to pause and admire. Some cities, towns and villages will require that splendour to be discovered, while others have beauty in abundance. Practically every street of this stunning mediaeval city radiates charm and elegance; it is without doubt a photographer's paradise. York's abundant historic structures, landmarks and architecture already possess the artistic visual qualities that photographers and artists pursue with great passion. It is often stated that to find a city's beauty you have to look upwards, but York disputes this statement and offers its guests beauty at both eye level and above.

We both hope that you enjoy viewing the images as much as we have enjoyed the challenge of ensuring that we capture the city in a manner that does justice to York's status, reputation and beauty.

Alistair and Jan Campbell

INTRODUCTION

Eboracum

'Place of the yew trees'

When exploring York's ancient structures, monuments and mediaeval streets, you tread on the heels of legendary emperors, kings, queens, lords, bishops, saints and martyrs. The city's mediaeval charm conceals a brutal history of bloodshed, sieges, religious persecution, plagues, floods and wars, all of which unite into an enthralling chronicle that spans almost 2,000 years and begins with the invasion of the Roman Ninth Legion in AD 71.

The confluence of the Rivers Ouse and Foss was recognised as a strategic military position for a Roman fortification that would provide garrisoned security against the marauding Celtic tribes known as the Brigantes. *Eboracum* – place of the yew trees – eventually became the Roman capital of the north.

The tactical importance of *Eboracum* was confirmed firstly by Saxon occupation, then Viking and Norman invasions. Under the Saxons *Eboracum* became *Eoforwic,* which in turn was superseded by the Viking title of *Jorvik.*

Invasion, religious reformation and persecution, the Dissolution of the Monasteries, civil war and industrial expansion are all part of a history that transcends Roman, Saxon, Viking, Norman, Mediaeval, Tudor, Stuart, Georgian and Victorian eras to the present. Throughout this period York has been witness to many momentous events which confirm that the history of York is a huge part of the history of England.

With over four million visitors each year, York owes much of its popularity as one of Britain's most favoured tourist destinations to its enthralling history. With such great heritage the city offers visitors and residents a legacy of ancient landmarks and traditions. York's streets and city walls contain mediaeval architecture, some of which has survived complete for over seven centuries, and many other much older visible foundations and structures.

Each page of *York City Beautiful* colourfully and aesthetically portrays a scene, landmark or tradition associated with this unique and historic city. Collectively the images and text offer an informative perspective and stunning portfolio which undoubtedly certifies that York is truly a City Beautiful.

THE CITY WALLS, BARS AND POSTERNS OF YORK

The construction of York's walled defence and fortification began with the arrival of the Roman Ninth Legion in AD 71. In order to establish a secure foothold in the north of England and protect themselves against the occupying Celtic tribes known as the Brigantes, the invading Romans constructed a fort (*castra*) occupying approximately 50 acres of land on the banks of the River Ouse. This rectangular settlement was initially surrounded by walls or mounds of an earthen rampart topped with timber palisades. It was not until the second and third centuries that the wooden defences were replaced with stone ramparts. Only a small proportion of the original Roman walls are still visible and integral to what is considered as England's longest surviving length of mediaeval walls.

From its original Roman origins, the walls' infrastructure, path and access routes have been subjected to many alterations. Almost three miles in length and enclosing an inner city area that exceeds 260 acres, the original mediaeval wall included four bars (gateways), posterns (or secondary gates) and a series of interval towers.

Strolling around the walled circuit is a popular leisure pursuit with both local residents and visitors alike. This Grade I listed and Scheduled Ancient Monument attracts over one million people every year. The route offers various joining and exit points and is normally closed to public access during the hours of darkness or in icy conditions. In addition to exploring the history and heritage associated with this mediaeval wall, the elevated position of the walled walkway offers stunning 360-degree vistas of the city and its outskirts.

The following images and information are only a portion of the scenes and history that can be discovered during a stroll along the entire length of the walled circuit. Although not intended as a comprehensive guide, the images and information are presented from a clockwise tour of the walls and begin at Bootham Bar.

An evening view of Exhibition Square with Bootham Bar and York Minster in the background. Slightly confusingly, a bar in York is a gateway and the name comes from their association with the barring of entry to the city. The bars initially served to both secure the city's inner boundaries from attack and collect tolls from tradesmen entering the city to sell their wares.

BOOTHAM BAR

Bootham Bar gateway was constructed on, or very near, the site of one of the original Roman entrance gates to the city. Some of the gate's construction materials may have been from former Roman structures. Although the mediaeval gateway has changed over the centuries, the archway is reputed to date from the 11th century, with the remaining masonry dating from approximately the 14th century onwards. A 'great door knocker' is believed to have been attached to the entrance oak doors so that any Scotsman who wished to enter the city could use the knocker to gain the Lord Mayor's permission. The site has also been subjected to siege damage and was used to display the severed heads of traitors. Unfortunately, in an act of local planning folly, the bar's barbican was demolished in 1832.

Bootham Bar viewed from High Petergate.

ROBIN HOOD TOWER

Rebuilt in 1889 on the site of an earlier tower, the design of Robin Hood Tower is not believed to be an accurate representation of its predecessor, but rather what the Victorians believed a mediaeval tower should look like. This large circular tower sports a number of cruciform arrow slits, while the platform also offers an excellent elevated view of the surrounding area.

Wooden benches allow an opportunity for a period of contemplation while admiring the views.

Wall route from Bootham Bar to Monk Bar.

A cruciform arrow slit.

The wall route from Bootham Bar to Monk Bar, and beyond, offers superb elevated views of York Minster, some of which are almost uninterrupted, while other perspectives provide glimpses through the adjacent garden shrubbery of those fortunate to reside in this beautiful area.

MONK BAR

Dating from the early 14th century, Monk Bar is the tallest and most ornate of the four principal city bars. Despite the loss of its barbican in 1825, it is the only gateway in York to have retained a working portcullis, which was last lowered and raised in 1953 to commemorate the coronation of Queen Elizabeth II. Now the home of The Richard III Museum, the association with King Richard III is, it is believed, that he personally ordered and paid for the construction of the top storey of this four-storey structure. Like a small fortress, if breached the structural design of Monk Bar enabled each floor to be independently defended.

Stone figures stand hurling stones from the top of the outward facing Monk Bar towers.

Goodramgate view of Monk Bar.

THE RICHARD III MUSEUM

Providing a concise history of King Richard III, the museum also offers visitors an opportunity to bear witness to a mock trial in which Richard III is accused of ordering the execution of his two nephews, Edward V and Richard, Duke of York - the Princes in the Tower - both of whom had a much stronger claim to the English throne than Richard.

Utilised as a prison during the 16th century, visitors can now explore the tiny prison cells and inspect the ancient lifting mechanism of the working portcullis. The two rooms above the central arch were also periodically let as residential dwellings until 1914.

A wax model of Richard III with his standard in the background.

The interior vaulted roof architecture and one of the prison cell entrances.

The portcullis lifting and lowering mechanism.

HARLOT HILL TOWER

A view of the wall route from Monk Bar, with Harlot Hill Tower in the distant background.

Additional path reference plaques also remind visitors that they are in the vicinity of a key historical structure.

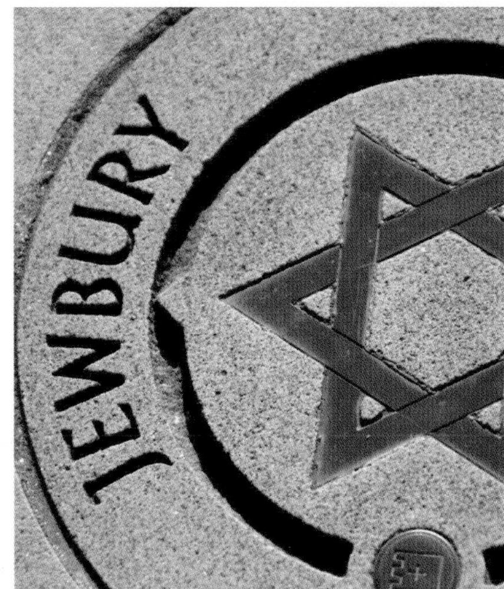

RED TOWER

Leaving this elevated section of wall at Layerthorpe Bridge, the route along Foss Island Road to the Red Tower was once under water. When the Normans deliberately dammed the River Foss at its juncture with the River Ouse, a defensive water barrier was formed, which did not require walls. As a result of the damming, a pool of fresh water was also created and became a royal preserve for fish and waterfowl know as King's Fishpool.

The Grade II listed Victorian Refuse Destructor Chimney, off Foss Island Road en route to the Red Tower.

Constructed from red brick rather than stone, the Red Tower was built in 1490 as a watchtower on the edge of the King's Fishpool. Eventually, the pool began to silt, creating a marshy area known as Foss Island. Draining of the marshes in the mid-19th century buried the Red Tower's foundations below ground level and attributes to the tower's squat appearance.

The wall route near the Red Tower.

Red Tower.

WALMGATE BAR

The most easterly of the four bars, Walmgate Bar is the only gateway to have retained a 14th-century, outer defensive barbican - it is also believed to be the only city gateway in England with a barbican. In addition, the 12th-century inner gateway, portcullis and 15th-century inner oak doors perhaps make it the most complete and authentic structure of the four principal mediaeval gateways. The bar was subject to fire damage during a tax riot in 1489 and also survived fierce attack and heavy gun bombardment from the Parliamentarian Army during the 1644 Civil War Siege of York. On the opposite side to the barbican, the bar supports the addition of a 16th-century Elizabethan wooden dwelling which had been let for residential use until 1957. Like the other bars, Walmgate Bar was also used for the gruesome purpose of displaying the severed heads of traitors on spikes.

Walmgate Bar with its surviving barbican.

Walmgate Bar and barbican viewed from the wall.

FISHERGATE BAR

At one time there may have been a small prison attached to Fishergate Bar, but as it is the least well preserved of the city gateways it is difficult to verify its original size and style. Badly damaged by fire during a riot in 1489, the bar was bricked up until its restoration in the early 18th century.

Fishergate Bar, with a city of York coat of arms and an inscription.

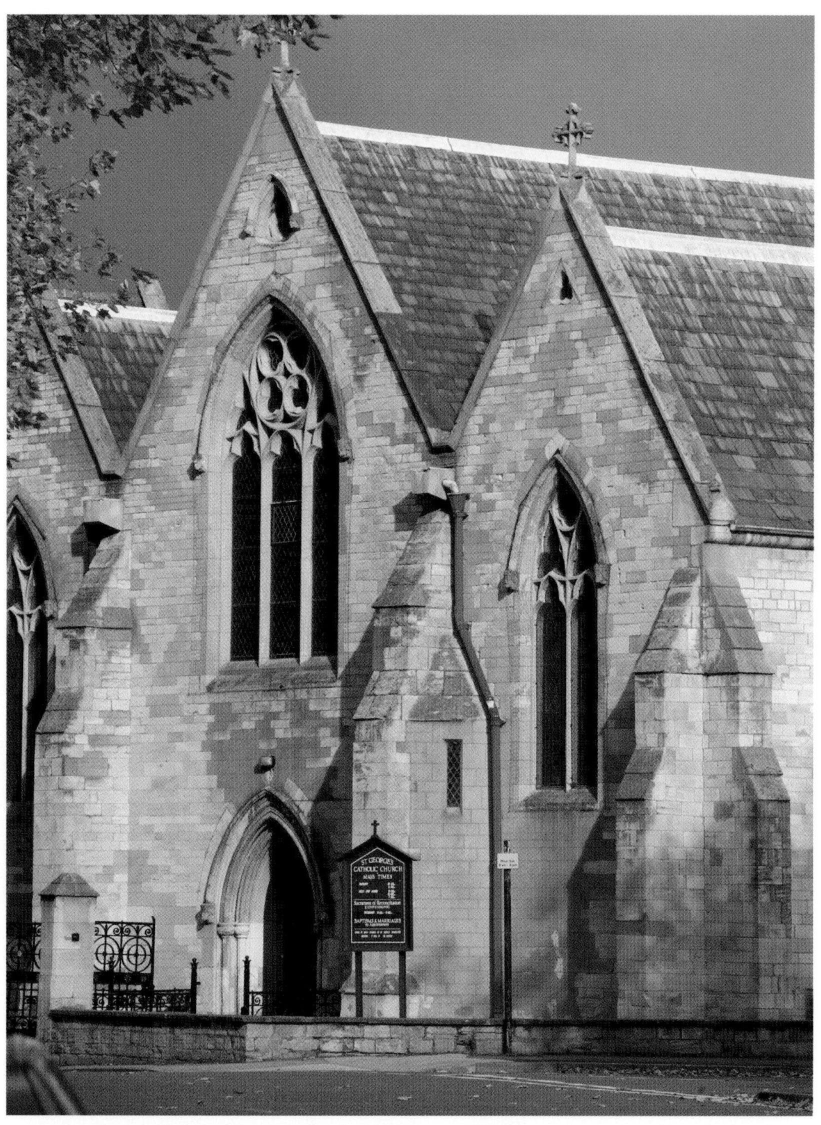

Just visible from Fishergate Bar is St George's Catholic Church, which was designed by Charles and Joseph Hansom in 1850 – Joseph Hansom was also responsible for the design of the popular Hansom Cab. St George's was built to serve the religious needs of an expanding Irish Catholic community, who had fled from Ireland's Potato Famine and had settled in the Walmgate area of York. Until St Wilfred's was built in Duncombe Place, St George's was the only Catholic cathedral church for the whole of Yorkshire.

FISHERGATE POSTERN TOWER

Fishergate Postern Tower was constructed very early in the 16th century as a replacement for the former Talkan Tower. The requirement for this newer tower may have originated from the bricking up of Fishergate Bar after riot damage. When constructed, the embankment of the River Foss was originally adjacent to the tower, but over the centuries the river has subsided to its current position. Other than the addition of a roof in 1740, there has been little if any change to the structural appearance of this tower.

Travel from Fishergate Postern Tower to the next section of the wall at Baile Hill is via a road that runs parallel to the castle complex. The route also passes over both the Rivers Foss and Ouse via Castle Mills Bridge and the 19th-century Thomas Page-designed Skeldergate Bridge.

Periodic rooftop views of the York Minster Central Tower provide wall explorers with a reassuring orientation point.

Viewed from Castle Mills Bridge is the River Foss, with the surviving castle walls and Debtors' Prison in the background.

The wall route near Micklegate Bar.

MICKLEGATE BAR

Possibly named after a Viking translation of 'Great Street', Micklegate Bar is considered to be the most prominent entrance gateway to the city. As the ancient primary route to and from the south, Micklegate Bar was nicknamed the 'Royal Gateway' where – in an ancient custom – visiting monarchs would traditionally stop at the gate to touch the State Sword. The lower stonework of the gateway dates from the 12th century, while the upper section was added during the 14th century. Throughout the centuries, the severed heads of traitor knights, lords and earls have adorned the roof battlements, where they have been left to rot for many years as a deterrent to any possible future conspirators. Unfortunately, it suffered the same architectural tragedy as Monk and Bootham Bars when its barbican was removed in the early 19th century – its portcullis was also removed around the same period. Currently housing the Micklegate Bar Museum, the upper floors of this four-storey gatehouse were also utilised as a family dwelling until 1838. The museum offers visitors the opportunity to explore the gate's history by allowing access to the various floors of the bar.

MICKLEGATE
BAR
MUSEUM

Micklegate Bar is adorned with a variety of stone figures, Royal coats of arms and crests.

An early morning view of one of York's most familiar vistas.

RAILWAY ARCHES

With the arrival of trains in the early 19th century, the Midland and Great North of England Railway Company demolished the walls and embankment at what is now known as Station Rise. The wall walkway was then initially restored with a single arch, allowing trains to access the station within the walls. As the train frequency increased, a second archway was added in 1845.

Railway arches now being used for road traffic.

BARKER TOWER

Built as part of the mediaeval city defences in the 14th century, Barker Tower - in conjunction with Lendal Tower on the opposite bank of the Ouse - controlled river access to and from the city. A large iron chain was suspended between the towers, which both strengthened the city defences and was used to extract tolls from transiting ferrymen. An identical defensive arrangement was also in operation further downstream at Davy Tower. The city sold the chains for common profit in the mid-16th century. The river entrance then had to be protected by canon mounted on boats during the Parliamentary and Royalist Civil War. Until the construction of Lendal Bridge in 1863, a ferry operated from Barker Tower.

LENDAL TOWER

Now being utilised as a luxury hotel complex, the 13th-century Lendal Tower was once part of the city wall defences. In the 16th century the structure was used as one of the country's earliest water towers, where it stored and pumped river water to city residents – or at least to those who could afford this luxury!

4

MULTANGULAR TOWER

Situated in the Museum Gardens, this 10-sided, nine-metre high defensive tower is believed to date from the year AD 210 and is one of the few sections of original Roman defensive wall structures that has survived. Only the first six metres of the tower's height are the original Roman masonry, while the larger upper blocks date from the mediaeval period. It is believed there was a similar tower at the other corner of the wall in what is now Feasegate Street.

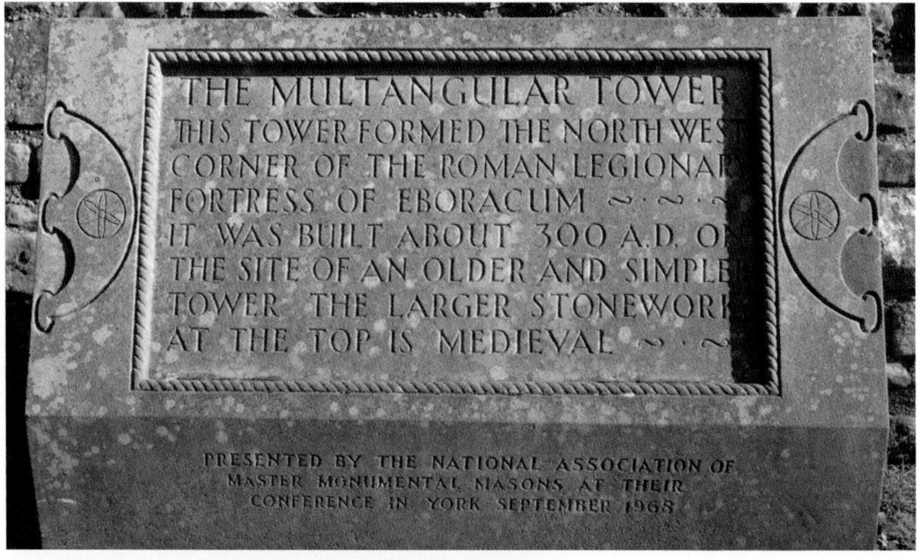

The tower information stone.

Remains of a Roman interval tower and the walled defences adjoining the Multangular Tower.

A walk around the inside of the Multangular Tower will reveal other Roman wall remnants and ancient stone coffins, which have been excavated from various locations around the city. Look carefully and you will see patched stonework from damage sustained by Parliamentary attackers during the Siege of York in 1644.

YORK MINSTER

Dominant and majestic over the city skyline are the towers of York Minster. As the seat of the Archbishop of York, this Church of England Cathedral and Minster is more formally acknowledged as the Cathedral and Metropolitan Church of St Peter in York. It is believed there were several religious structures preceding York Minster. From its humble seventh-century timber beginnings, each successive building grew in stature and importance. Equally, in turn, each succeeding structure was deliberately or accidentally damaged by invading factions, mishaps and neglect. By the time Walter de Grey was appointed the Archbishop of York in 1215, a large Norman church already sat on the site of today's York Minster and sections of the original Norman columns are still visible in the Minster's undercroft. Walter de Grey initiated a construction programme that was to last over 250 years and culminated in the completion of one of the largest Gothic cathedrals in Northern Europe. Archbishop de Grey's plan began with the building of the North and South Transepts, but he died in 1251 before their completion and was buried in the South Transept. Since its completion in 1472, other than modifications to how religious worship is performed, very little of the Minster's architectural fabric changed, that is until February 1829. Jonathan Martin deliberately started a fire in the Quire which resulted in the destruction of the entire east end roof and timber vault, including all the original quire furnishings. Martin insisted that God had instructed him to destroy the Minster and was convicted and found guilty of arson, which, if he had been sane, would have resulted in the death penalty. However, the jury decided that Jonathan Martin was of unsound mind, so he was sentenced to life imprisonment in an asylum. Although the damage was repaired, just over a decade later a second, but this time accidental, fire destroyed the nave roof.

Two further significant events in the 20th century again perilously threatened the Minster's future preservation. Firstly, a survey revealed that unless the building foundations were significantly strengthened then the central tower and roof were in danger of collapse. Underpinning work was completed in 1972 and offered archaeologists the opportunity to explore the foundations for further clues to the building's history. Indeed, during this work Roman foundations and columns were unearthed, which led

archaeologists to believe that the Minster had been constructed on top of the Roman Legionary Headquarters or *Principia*.

A major fire, caused by a lightning strike in 1984, badly damaged the South Transept roof – if you look closely, an assortment of scorched telltale signs from the disaster still remain. During restoration of the fire damaged roof it was decided to allow children to design six of the replacement bosses. A competition was held by the popular children's television programme *Blue Peter*. The winning designs included astronauts and the preservation of Henry VIII's recovered ship, the *Mary Rose*.

The former York Minster Library now being used as the Minster shop.

ROSE WINDOW

Sitting high above the South Transept, the masonry of the Rose Window was completed in the middle of the 13th century, with the outer stained glass panels being added over 250 years later in the early 16th century. With a diameter of almost seven metres, the images of red roses (House of Lancaster) and white roses (House of York) commemorate the end of the War of the Roses and the union of the Houses of Lancaster and York, which followed the marriage of Henry VII and Elizabeth of York in 1486. Added much later in 1793 were the brightly painted inner patterns which were created by William Peckitt. Heat from the 1984 lightning strike fire in the South Transept caused over 40,000 cracks in the famous Tudor Rose Window, and it took specialist glaziers two and a half years to repair and restore the damaged window.

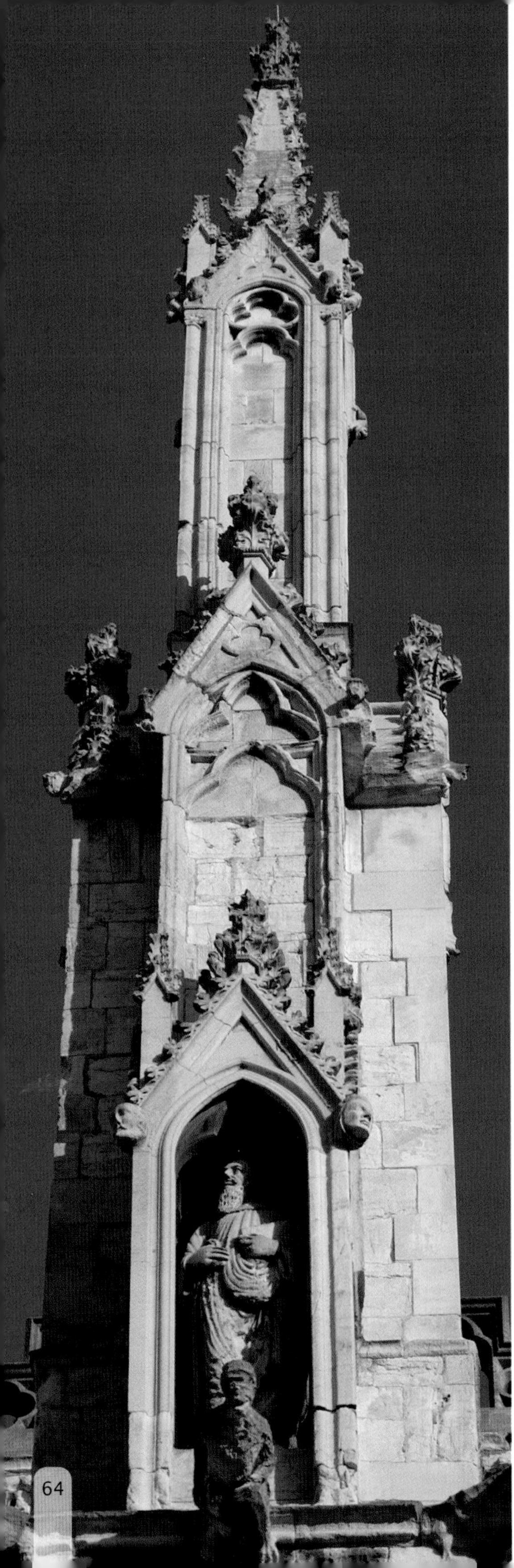

LVCE
DEMONST
VMBRA
IHS XP
X·XI·XII·I·II·III

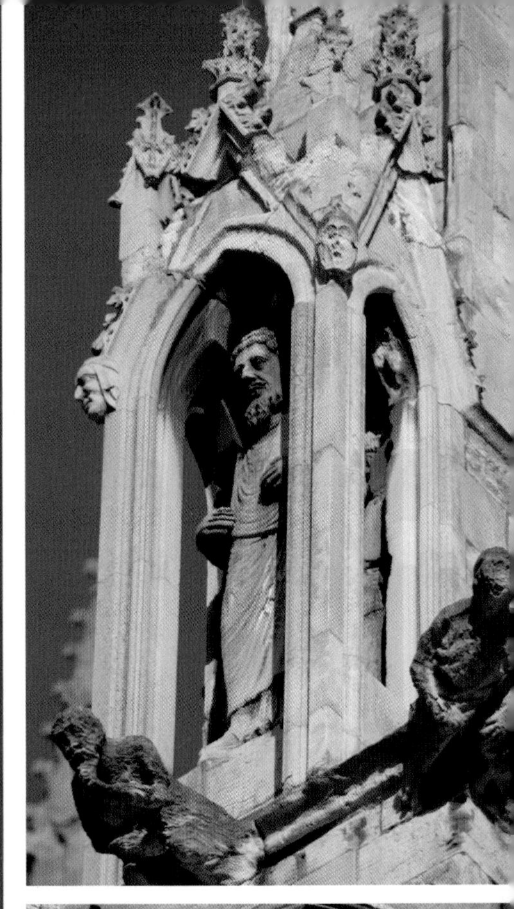

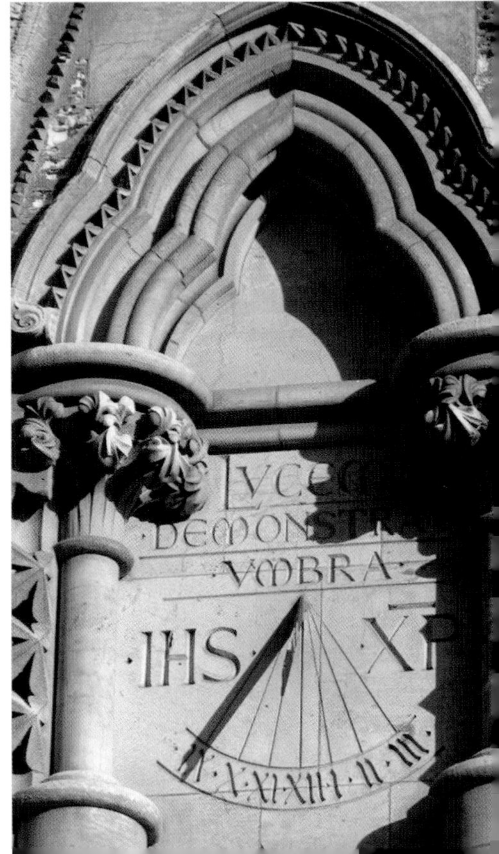

Views of York Minster at night.

NAVE

This large expanse was not used for services until the 19th century. As the widest Gothic nave in England, the area can seat almost 2,000 people. Although the nave aisles have vaulted stone roofs, the main roof is made from wood but is painted to give the impression of stone.

STAINED GLASS

With 128 glass windows and over two million individual pieces of glass, the Minster contains one of the best collections of stained glass in England.

The nave looking east towards the Quire Screen.

View of the nave and Great West Window.

GREAT WEST WINDOW

Nicknamed the Heart of Yorkshire, the Great West Window stonework was created by Master Mason Ivo de Raghton and dates from the early 14th century. The stained glass depicts a variety of Christian scenes, including the life of Christ and previous Archbishops of York. Some of the original scenes have been replaced over the centuries.

An external view of the Great West Window.

MINSTER ORGAN

Towering above the Quire Screen is the Minster organ which, over the centuries, has been subjected to many rebuilds, alterations and replacements.

FIVE SISTERS WINDOW

Dating from approximately 1260, the Five Sisters Window is said to contain over 100,000 individual pieces of glass and is the oldest of the Minster's great windows. Each of the five lancet windows is 16 metres high and contains patterns set in grey grisaille glass. The origin of the name Five Sisters is difficult to verify and there are several theories involving Cistercians, Charles Dickens and the local historian Francis Drake.

The North Transept, organ and Five Sisters Window.

CENTRAL TOWER

At a height of 60 metres and weighing approximately 16,000 tons, the Central Tower was completed in 1472.

NORTH TRANSEPT

Built in the same period as its neighbouring South Transept, the North Transept contains the Five Sisters Window. In addition to being used for exhibitions and performances, the space is also used to display Christmas nativity and Easter scenes.

The Central Tower with the North Transept.

QUIRE SCREEN

Directly below the Central Tower is the Quire Screen, which is decorated with stone carvings of England's kings – the name of each king is below the relevant statue.

The Quire Screen entrance.

The Quire Screen stone carvings of England's Kings.

QUIRE

Transiting through the Quire Screen leads you into the Quire with the magnificent backdrop of the Lady Chapel and Great East Window. Badly damaged by an arson attack in 1829, the Quire furnishings are Victorian replacements.

RESERVED FOR DEANERY

GREAT EAST WINDOW

Created by the glass painter John Thornton between 1405 and 1408, the Great East Window covers an area of almost 200 square metres and is said to be the 'single largest area of mediaeval glass in the world'. The window normally sits high above the Lady Chapel in the east end of the Minster, but as part of a major restoration project the window was removed in 2008. Work is expected to be complete within a decade and the cost of restoring the window will be approximately seven million pounds. Currently in its place is an immense representation of the original window, offering visitors an impressive vision of what the window will look like when it is returned to its former glory and location.

The Quire and Great East Window.

CHAPTER HOUSE

Connected to the Minster via the Vestibule, the octagonal-shaped Chapter House is said to contain some of the Minster's finest carvings and glass. Although construction of it began in 1260, it took 26 years to complete and it is still used for its original purpose - as a meeting place for the Dean and Chapter.

MINSTER CLOSE

Acting as a city within a city, Minster Close was once governed by its own laws, court and prison. The then Minster of St Peter was sheltered from the outside world by its private protective gates and walls. Although the walls and gates are now gone, the Minster still employs its own policemen, who are responsible for the security and protection of York Minster and the immediate surrounding area. A visit to York would not be complete without further exploration of this historic and picturesque precinct.

EMPEROR CONSTANTINE

Sculpted by Philip Jackson, a statue of Constantine the Great is located near the south door of the Minster. Constantine is believed to have been proclaimed Emperor on the spot that York Minster now stands. Although difficult to verify, Emperor Constantine is credited with being the first Roman Emperor to become a Christian. He, at the very least, was the first Emperor to tolerate and promote Christianity.

Located opposite the Constantine statue is a Roman column which was unearthed during the Minster's foundation underpinning programme in the 1960s.

DEAN'S PARK

Created in the early 19th century when ruined buildings were cleared from the area, Dean's Park is a tranquil spot that attracts many city workers and visitors for picnic lunches. At noon each day any quiet contemplation is briefly and pleasantly interrupted by the ring of the Minster's Great Peter Bell.

A view of the Minster from Dean's Park.

ST MICHAEL LE BELFREY

Standing in the shadows of York Minster is the early 16th-century St Michael le Belfrey. Open to visitors and worshippers on most days, the parish church was originally intended to serve the local parishioners who were not considered affluent enough to worship at the Minster. The notorious Guy Fawkes was baptised at the church in 1570.

MINSTER LIBRARY

Built as a private chapel for the Archbishop of York, the 13th-century building now houses the Minster archives and cathedral library, within which is a large collection of books and manuscripts, including ancient and rare publications. The library is occasionally open to the public for themed exhibitions.

In the vicinity of the Minster Library are the ruined remains of the arcading which originally formed a covered walkway between the Archbishop's Palace and his private chapel – now the library. The arcading contains the 2nd Division Kohima Memorial, which was unveiled by the Queen Mother in June 1987.

Aerial view of the Deanery and Minster Library, with the York City Walls in the background.

Built in 1940 as the home for the Dean of York, the Deanery is a relatively recent addition to the surrounding precinct.

TREASURER'S HOUSE

Sitting in the shadow of York Minster is the elegant, early 15th-century mansion which is named after the Treasurer of York Minster. The house was used in its treasury capacity until the mid 16th-century, when, after the reformation, it was sold for private ownership. In 1720 one of its owners divided the property in two, which separated Gray's Court and its courtyard from Treasurer's House. The house continued to be further divided until 1897, when one of its sections was purchased by Frank Green.

After acquiring all the house sections, Green restored the exterior and then fastidiously styled each room to display his collection of period furniture. On his retirement to Somerset in 1930, and under strict instructions that nothing was to be moved, Frank Green left the house and furniture to the National Trust.

There are many rumours that the house cellar is haunted by Roman soldiers, who have been seen marching through the cellar walls. The soldiers are said to be dirty, tired looking and only visible from the knees upwards. It was later discovered that a Roman road was buried under the house foundations. Managed by the National Trust, both the house and its cellars are open to visitors at specified times.

GRAY'S COURT

Originally part of the Treasurer's residence, Gray's Court is named after the generation of families who lived there for almost 200 years. Now a private residence, Gray's Court is not open to the public.

ST WILLIAM'S COLLEGE

Erected as a residential college for chantry priests of the Minster, this mid-15th-century building is named after Archbishop William FitzHerbert, who was canonised in 1227. In 1154 a vast crowd is said to have gathered to greet the archbishop on his return from a meeting with the Pope in Rome. A wooden bridge over the Ouse collapsed and many of the crowd fell into the river, but no one drowned and the miracle was attributed to William. The archbishop died soon after this incident and his tomb is located within the Minster. Sold after the Reformation, the building has been used for both residential and commercial purposes. This fascinating building was restored in the 20th century and is now used as a conference and event venue. St William's College café and restaurant is open to the public.

YORK MINSTER
CONFERENCE
& BANQUETING
CENTRE

THE STREETS OF YORK

The names of many of York's streets, lanes and snickleways (small passageways) are usually linked to their history. The following images are only a small representation of the fine architecture, scenes and landmarks that are associated with this ancient, impressive and proud city. Personal exploration and research will undoubtedly reveal other architectural, historic and landmark treasures.

CASTLEGATE

Fairfax House is described as one of the finest Georgian townhouses in England. Built in 1762 for Viscount Fairfax, the interior of this 18th-century building was designed by John Carr. Now home to the renowned Noel Terry Collection of English furniture and clocks, the house is managed by the York Civic Trust and is open to the public at times specified by the trust.

At 47 metres high, York St Mary's has the tallest steeple in York. This mediaeval church is now being used as a contemporary arts centre.

Fairfax House.

CLIFFORD STREET

Victorian architecture of the Law Courts on Clifford Street.

COPPERGATE AND THE JORVIK VIKING CENTRE

Excavations by the York Archaeological Trust on the site of a demolished confectionery factory in Coppergate led to the discovery of an extensive, well-preserved collection of over 40,000 objects relating to the Viking era. During a three-year period of excavations, which began in 1979, it was discovered that the damp peat-type earth of the site had helped to preserve many of the findings that are now displayed at the Jorvik Viking Centre. Visitors to this highly popular attraction are transported on a tour of reconstructed Viking streets and scenes that represent the era at precisely 5.30pm on 25 October AD 975. An innovative journey through history is complemented by interactive displays and Viking-clad characters that are eager to demonstrate their trades, skills and way of life.

Two Vikings, Sigwulf and Leif, playing the board game Hnefatafl.

ALL SAINTS PAVEMENT CHURCH

Although there has been a religious structure on this site since before the Norman Conquest, the All Saints Pavement Church dates from the 14th century. Its lantern tower was added in approximately the early 15th century - the light from the tower was supposedly a night guide for travellers approaching from the dangers of the surrounding countryside.

An evening view of the Coppergate shopping centre with the lantern tower of the All Saints Pavement Church in the background.

All Saints Pavement Church.

DUNCOMBE PLACE

Leading directly from Museum Street to York Minster is Duncombe Place. This early 18th-century townhouse, known as the Red House, was constructed for Sir William Robinson, who was the Lord Mayor of York in 1700. Now an Aladdin's cave of antique treasures, the house is currently known as the Antiques Centre.

The Red House still retains its city coat of arms above the main entrance.

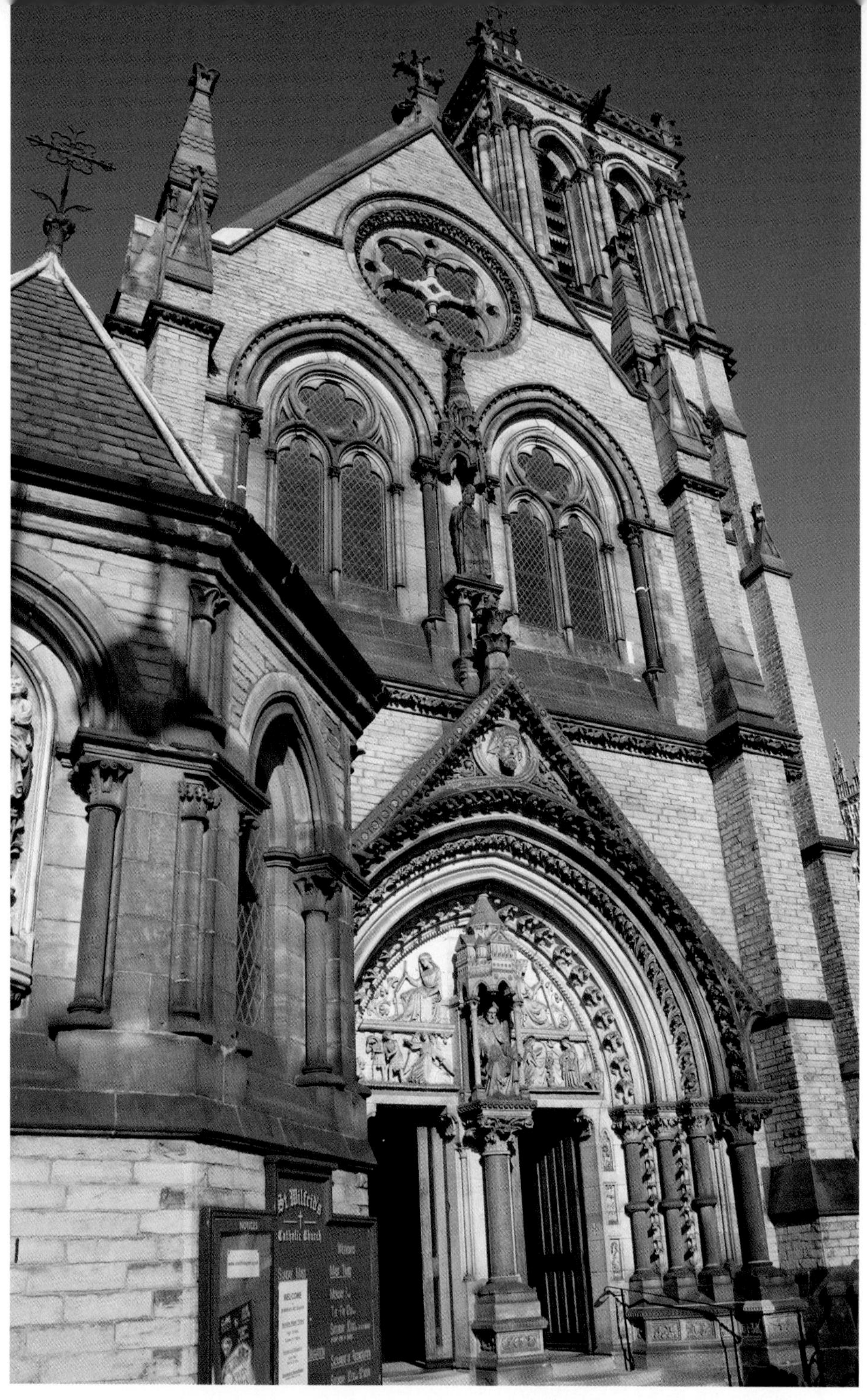

Designed in a Gothic revival style by George Goldie, St Wilfred's Roman Catholic Church foundation stone was laid in April 1862. The building was completed two years later at a cost of £10,000.

The George Frederick Bodley-designed Boer War Memorial at Duncombe Place, with the bell tower of York Minster in the background.

FOSSGATE

The arched and balustraded Foss Bridge over the River Foss was built in the early 19th century.

MERCHANT ADVENTURERS' HALL

This mediaeval oak-framed building was constructed on the site of a former Norman mansion in the mid-14th century. The Merchant Adventurers' Hall was initially a religious institution known as the Guild of Our Lord, but later became a meeting place for the Guild of Merchant Adventurers. The guild would conduct business transactions and socialise in the great hall, pray in the chapel and attend to the needs of the poor in the undercroft. This Grade I listed and Scheduled Ancient Monument is open to the public and is also available for private hire.

The Merchant Adventurers of England coat of arms above the Fossgate entrance to the Merchant Adventurers' Hall.

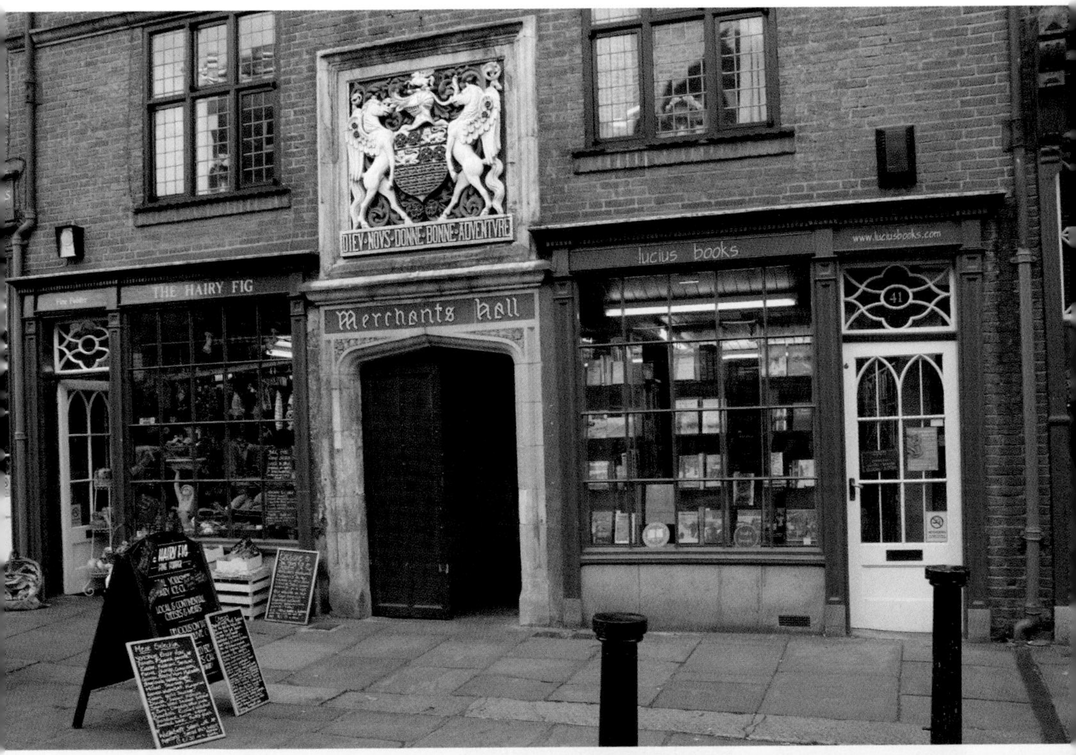
DIEV NOVS DONNE BONNE ADVENTVRE
THE HAIRY FIG
Merchants Hall
lucius books
www.luciusbooks.com
41

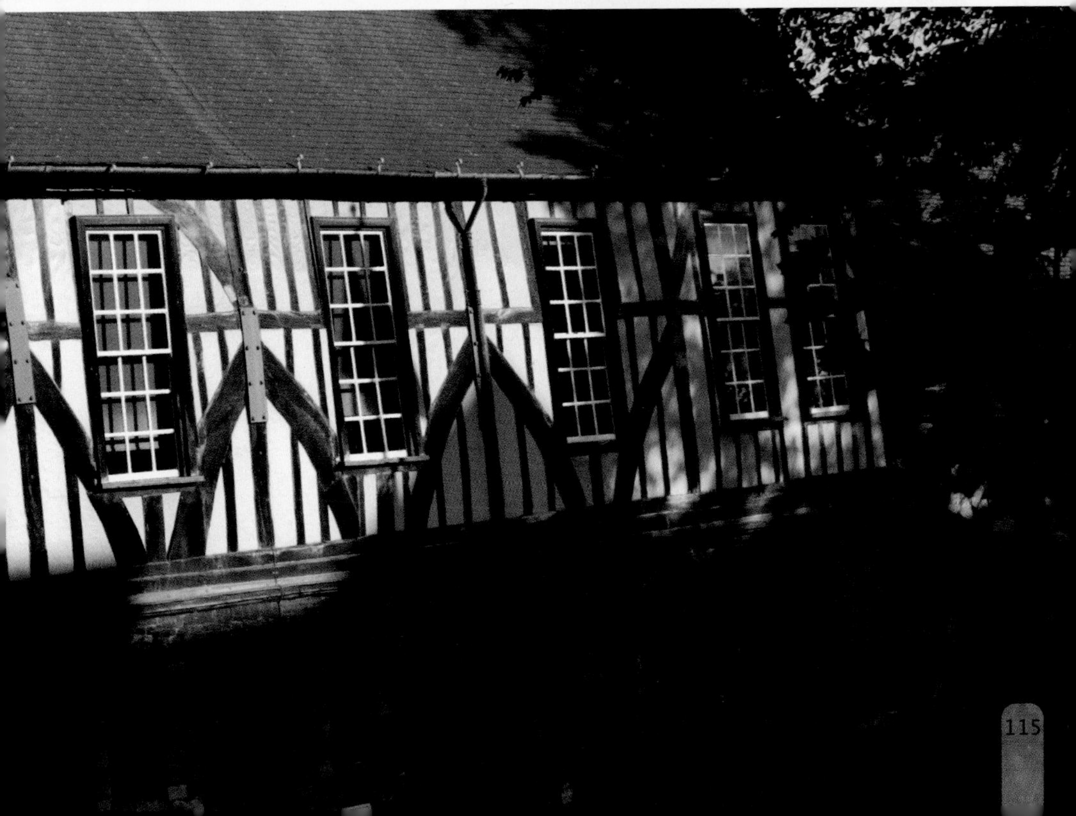

MINSTER GATES

A former entrance to the mediaeval precinct of York Minster, the north end of this short quaint street is framed by the South Transept of York Minster. In an area that has strong traditional links with book sales and printing, an extensive range of specialist and general literature can still be perused and purchased. Previously, Minster Gates has been known as Bookland Lane and Bookbinder's Alley.

Leaning against a pile of books above the junction of Minster Gates and High Petergate is a statue of Minerva, the Roman goddess of wisdom.

PETERGATE

York Minster is dedicated to St Peter; therefore, it can be safely assumed that both High and Low Petergate are so-named because of their close proximity to the Minster.

Starting from Bootham Bar, High Petergate intersects the junction of Minster Gates and Stonegate, before converging with Low Petergate and ending at King's Square. Containing a complex mixture of hotels, dining establishments, public houses, shops and historical buildings, this fascinating street is overshadowed by the magnificent structure of York Minster.

Guy Fawkes, the notorious leader of the Gun Powder Plot, was supposedly born in this house, which is now the Guy Fawkes Inn.

Low Petergate.

SHAMBLES

Mentioned in the 11th-century *Domesday Book*, the Shambles is one of York's oldest streets and is reputedly one of Europe's best preserved examples of a mediaeval street.

As one of York's most popular street destinations with tourists, the Shambles now contains a quaint array of small independent retail outlets, including cafés, restaurants, curiosity and gift shops. This now picturesque scene of a narrow street with overhanging timber-framed buildings contrasts dramatically with the blood, carnage and smell that one would have experienced in a bygone era, when animals were slaughtered, prepared and sold in the street's numerous butcher's shops. Once known as the Great Flesh Shambles, the name is said to originate from the mediaeval term *flesshammel* or flesh-shelves. Near the Shambles was a bull ring, where animals would be purchased before being taken to the rear of the owner's shop and slaughtered for resale. Any unwanted offal would be thrown into the centre groves of the narrow street and periodically swept away by water. The keeping, slaughtering and disposing of the animals would have, at the very least, proved pungent. Some of the shops still retain the overhanging hooks and wide window ledge shelves, where the meat would have been displayed for sale many decades ago.

CHOCOLATE HEAVEN
Handmade Chocolates
Tea Rooms

At the time of writing, only one butcher's shop has survived, which is located in the adjacent lane of Little Shambles.

LITTLE SHAMBLES

SAINT MARGARET CLITHEROW

Born in the middle of the 16th century, St Margaret Clitherow married a wealthy butcher and resided in York's Shambles. Also known as The Pearl of York and The Martyr of York, Margaret's life and fate are well documented. During this era of Catholic persecution under the reign of Queen Elizabeth I, Margaret allowed her house to be used as a shelter for priests. This commitment to her Catholic Christian faith ensured that she suffered long periods of imprisonment. Despite Margaret's attempts to keep her Christian beliefs reasonably covert, she was arrested for the final time in March 1586. A refusal to plead guilty to the crime of harbouring priests and hearing Mass, which may have incriminated her children, resulted in the sentence of *peine forte et dure* or death by crushing. At Ouse Bridge tollbooth on Good Friday 1586, Margaret Clitherow endured a slow and painful end to her life after being crushed to death by a heavy weight. A house in the Shambles now contains a shrine to St Margaret Clitherow.

ST HELEN'S SQUARE

A focal point of interconnecting streets, St Helen's Square is flanked at one end by Mansion House and the Guildhall, while at the other stands the mediaeval St Helen's Church and Betty's Café. Extensive 18th-century redevelopment of the area required the then St Helen's churchyard to be removed to form a paved public square.

ST HELEN'S CHURCH

With a façade that dates from the 12th century, the mediaeval St Helen's Church may be even older. The church was closed and partly demolished in the 16th century, but because of its prominent location within the city it was ordered to be restored. This was not the last time that this small parish church was to come under threat of closure, but despite centuries of financial hardship and World War Two bomb damage, the church continues to stand proud in its rightful position overlooking the majestic St Helen's Square and Mansion House.

Since opening its doors in the late 1930s, 'tea at Betty's Café Tea Rooms' has developed into one of York's most enjoyable traditions. The immense windows allow its patrons to admire the hustle and bustle of St Helen's Square, while sitting comfortably in the café's elegant surroundings.

EVELYN

ST LEONARD'S PLACE

The Patrick Gwynne-designed 1960s foyer is a modern embellishment to the historic Victorian Gothic-styled York Theatre Royal. The theatre is built over the 12th-century vaults of St Leonard's Hospital.

The Abbot of St Mary's house was renamed King's Manor after the Dissolution of the Monasteries in the 16th century. Throughout the centuries the plot has been extensively altered and extended. This former 16th-century headquarters for the Council of the North later became the Yorkshire School for the Blind and is now part of the University of York.

STONEGATE

A quaint selection of shops, cafés, public houses, restaurants and high-quality retailers line the Stonegate route north from St Helen's Square towards Petergate and Minster Gate. It has been said that the street name originates from the vast quantity of Tadcaster stone that was transported from the riverbank to York Minster via Stonegate. Perhaps more simply the street is named after its cobbled walkways. This attractive street has retained much of its mediaeval charm, making it a popular tourist route to and from York Minster.

The Printer's Devil indicates the site of a former print works – printers' apprentices were known as Printer's Devils.

TIONAL
ALES
YE OLDE STARRE INNE
YORK'S OLDEST LICENSED INN 1644
Cavendish
Antiques
& Collectors
Centre
Inglis
& Son
(JEWELLERS) LTD
CAFÉ

YORK CASTLE

A direction sign from York Minster to the castle.

CASTLE GREEN

Known by a variety of pseudonyms including the Eye of York, Eye of the Ridings or Castle Green, this green civic space is surrounded on all sides by historic buildings and structures. York Castle complex contains an ancient motte castle and castle walls; debtors and female prison, both of which now house the York Castle Museum; and the former County Court House, which now serves as York Crown Court.

CLIFFORD'S TOWER

Under the order of William the Conqueror in 1068, a motte with a wooden palisade was constructed on the site that is now known as Clifford's Tower. In 1069, during a counter-attack by the Danes, this structure was destroyed but was immediately rebuilt and strengthened by William I. The motte castle was originally intended to offer protection against an anti-Norman uprising and act as a centre for enforcing William's Harrying of the North campaign. Although the castle and motte retained its timber defences for some years, further accidental and deliberate incidents destroyed various versions of the fortification. One event of particular note occurred during the Crusades under the banner of Richard the Lionheart in the late 12th century, when there was little tolerance of non-Christian beliefs throughout Europe and England. In 1190, following anti-Jewish riots in London, King's Lynn and Norwich, the Jewish community in York sought refuge in the tower from an angry crowd. Feeling so threatened in the ensuing siege, many of the inhabitants, rather than surrender themselves to the awaiting mob, burnt their protective fortification to the ground and decided to die by their own hands, while those who did surrender were slaughtered. In the middle of the 13th century Henry III instigated the building of a stone castle. Since this more sturdy construction, Clifford's Tower has undergone further siege, fire, water damage, restoration and even theft of its masonry - for which its perpetrator, Robert Redhead, was sentenced to death. Originally named King's Tower or High Tower, there are at least two versions of how it

obtained its current name. The first is attributed to Henry Clifford, the then Earl of Cumberland, who was garrisoned at the castle and whose family crest appears above its entrance, while the second version states that the tower is named after Sir Roger de Clifford, whose body was hung from the castle walls for treason by order of Edward II. The quatrefoil design of the tower is said to be unusual for England and is certainly the most complete remaining example of this style of defence in the country. Clifford's Tower is one of two castles in the area and although the mound of the second castle is still very visible, and not far away, there is no trace of its fortification.

Clifford's Tower has been used as a garrison, mint, prison and is now one of York's most popular tourist destinations. Managed by English Heritage, a visit to the castle offers an insight into its enthralling and bloody history with, as an additional bonus, its battlements providing sweeping panoramic views of the city and its surrounds. This monument's historical inheritance serves to verify a quotation stating that 'the history of York is the history of England'.

The king's crest and the Clifford family crest above the tower entrance.

FEMALE PRISON

Completed in 1780, the Female Prison is in a similar style to the John Carr-designed County Court House which sits opposite. Built to cope with the increasing work of the courts, the prison also housed an infirmary and later a chapel. Two new wings designed by Peter Atkinson Senior were added in 1802. The building now forms an integral part of the Castle Museum.

CASTLE MUSEUM

CASTLE MUSEUM

MUSEUM

COUNTY COURT HOUSE

This Georgian period building was designed by the architect John Carr, a former Lord Mayor of the city. Carr was also responsible for many other Yorkshire public and private structures, including the interior design of the nearby Fairfax House. After being completed in 1777, over two centuries later the County Court House is still being used for its original purpose of justice, but it now has the title of York Crown Court.

Views of the former County Court House with Clifford's Tower in the background.

A rear view of the County Court House architecture.

Lady Justice and unicorn statue.

COUNTY GAOL (DEBTORS' PRISON)

York County Gaol was completed in the very early 18th century and was later named the Debtors' Prison after the transgression of some of its inmates. The gaol also housed criminals who had been convicted of other types of offences, and guests included the notorious highwayman Dick Turpin. Debtors were divided into three classes and occupied the upper floors of the prison, while common criminals were imprisoned on the ground floor. The prison governor and the chapel were also originally housed in this building. It is difficult to verify the architect of this fine English Baroque-style building, but some sources attribute the design to a local lawyer named William Wakefield. Although modern in comparison to other similar institutes of the period, the elegance of the façade hid the overcrowded living conditions that prisoners endured inside, as inmates suffered suffocation, disease and beatings.

All three buildings later became integrated into a more substantial penal detention complex. This larger Victorian prison lasted from 1835 until its demolition in 1934, but fortunately all three of the 18th-century buildings and Clifford's Tower were spared. Both the former Debtors' and Female Prisons are now home to the Castle Museum.

The Debtors' Prison clock tower.

An evening view of the Debtors' Prison, County Court House and the Castle Museum entrance.

CASTLE MUSEUM

Founded by Dr John Kirk, the Castle Museum was first opened in 1938. Dr Kirk was an ardent collector of period items. As his collection outgrew both his personal accommodation and a local exhibition hall in nearby Pickering, he offered the items to anyone who would house and display them in an appropriate manner. York City Council had demolished the Victorian prison complex from the castle grounds in 1934 and offered Dr Kirk the Female Prison as a potential location to house his collection. Due to the popularity, success and increasing number of museum exhibits, the museum expanded into the Debtors' Prison in 1952. From its inception, the Castle Museum has successfully strived to provide an entertaining and educational exhibition that relates to everyday life. Indeed, the authenticity of the Victorian Street, Kirkgate, is both globally renowned and unsurpassed. Its cobbled street is lined with an array of shops, all of which have been dismantled and moved from their original location and carefully reconstructed in Kirkgate to provide an accurate and realistic vision of Victorian life. Creative lighting effects and staged, costumed characters allow visitors to experience the sights and sounds of a whole day.

Kirkgate is named after the museum's benefactor and founder Dr John Kirk.

A friendly and informative shopkeeper in one of the Victorian shops.

The Moorland Cottage and the more opulent Victorian Parlour are an excellent way to compare the contrast between the domestic lives of the middle and working classes during the mid-19th century.

A 17th-century dining room.

This more modern, mid-20th-century family sitting room may rekindle the memories of some visitors.

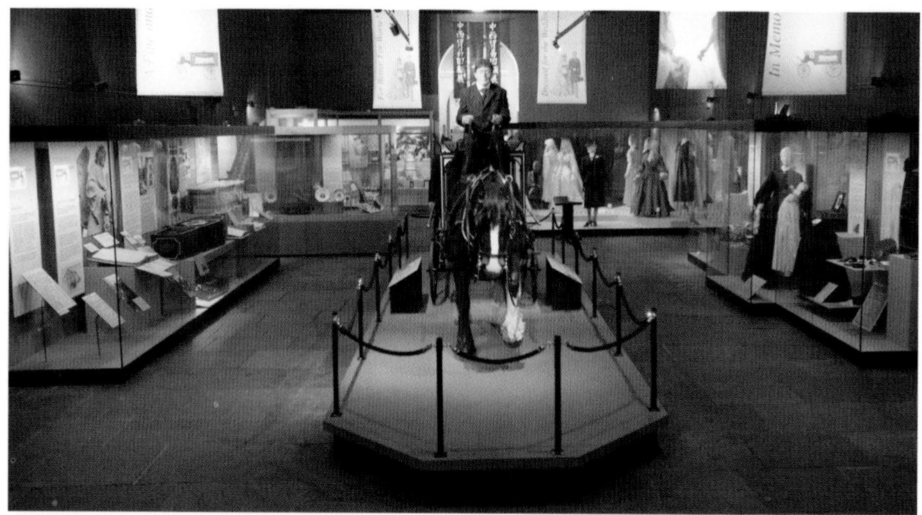

The Cradle to Grave exhibition housed in the former Female Prison Chapel.

The history of the actual buildings is not forgotten and few visitors forego the opportunity to visit the Condemned Cell, where the highwayman Dick Turpin allegedly spent his last days before being hanged at York's Knavesmire on 7 April 1739. Although guilty of more serious offences, Turpin was actually hanged for the crime of horse stealing not highway robbery.

The Condemned Cell.

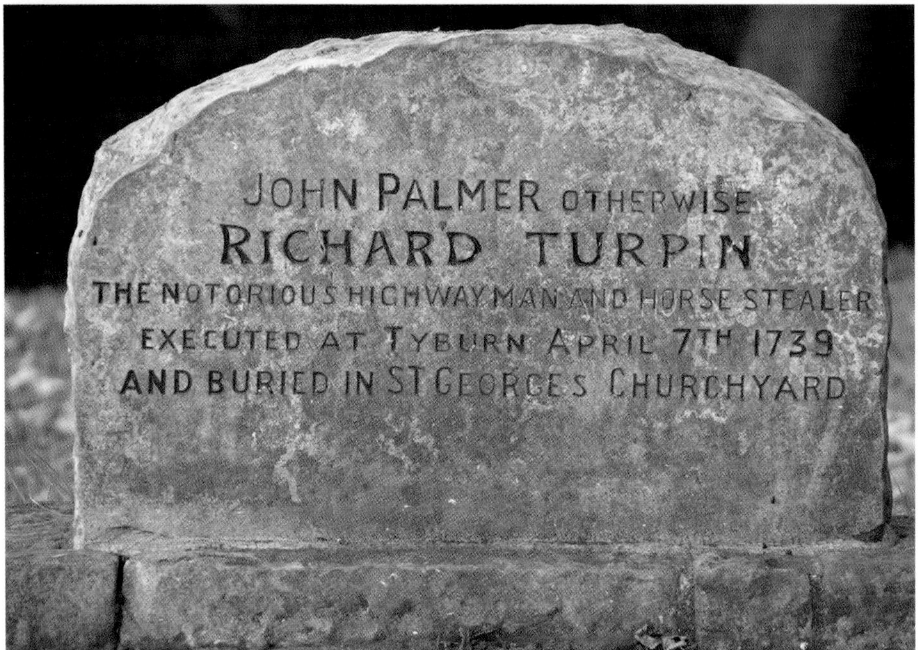

Buried in nearby St George's Churchyard, Dick Turpin's gravestone is still visible today.

Permanent exhibitions are regularly complemented with innovative temporary displays and demonstrations. This sixties collection explores an exciting period of music, space exploration, fashion and many other facets of this highly influential decade.

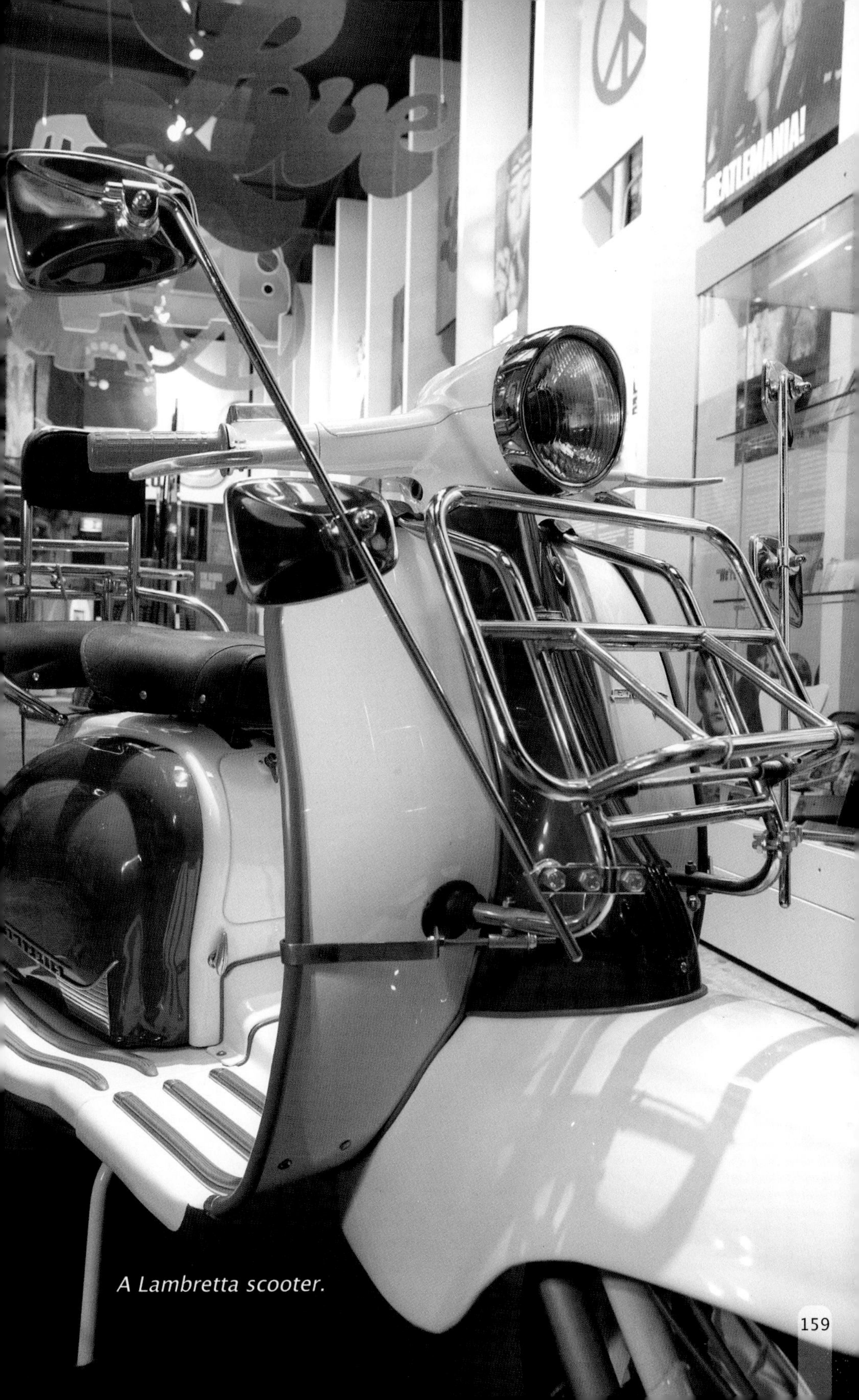

A Lambretta scooter.

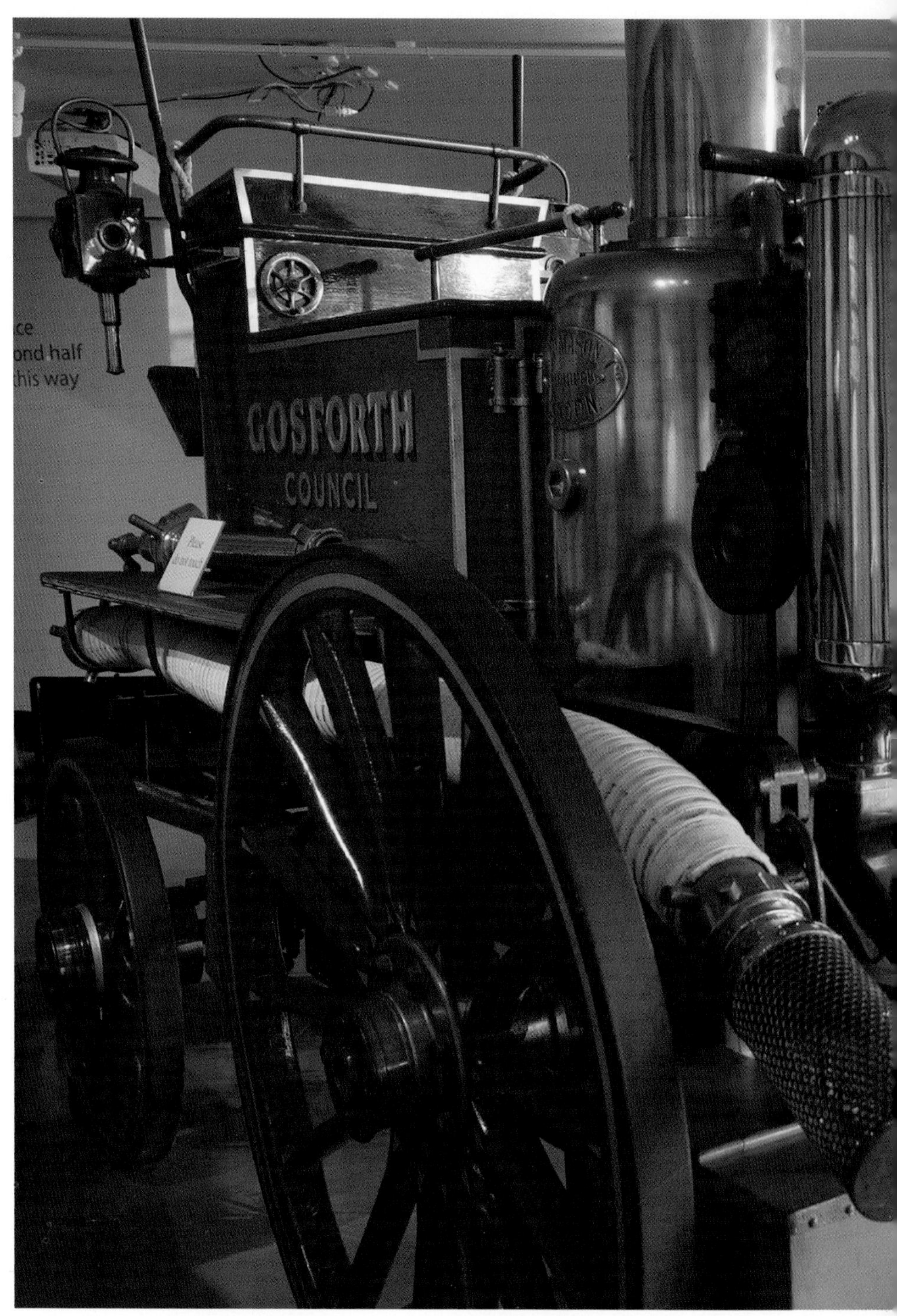
GOSFORTH
COUNCIL

Once owned by Gosforth Council and then the York chocolate confectioner Rowntree's Co Ltd, this superb example of the 1905 Shand Mason & Co fire engine now adorns the entrance hall and gift shop of the York Castle Museum.

MUSEUM GARDENS

Located in the grounds of the former St Mary's Abbey, this 10-acre botanical garden was designed in a 'gardenesque style' by the landscape architect Sir John Murray Naysmith. Gardenesque is a style which is described as artistic rather than natural, with plants or planting patterns that would, perhaps, not naturally be associated with that particular landscape or environment.

Although the garden was established in the early 19th century, a stroll around this picturesque area will reveal a surprising number of buildings, structures and ruins which date from the Roman era onwards. A popular lunchtime haunt for city workers, its secluded grounds offer both visitors and locals welcome respite from the adjacent bustling city centre.

YORKSHIRE MUSEUM

This Grade I listed building was designed in the classical style by the architect William Wilkins. Completed in 1829 and opening its doors the following year, the Yorkshire Museum is one of the first purpose-built museums in the country. Constructed over a proportion of St Mary's Abbey building foundations (which can still be seen in the basement of the museum), its archaeological collection includes impressive objects relating to the Roman, Anglo-Saxon and Viking periods, most of which have been discovered in the city and its rural surrounds. This intriguing and rare collection offers a vivid insight into York's rich history and heritage. The archaeology collection is complemented by other permanent geology and natural history exhibitions, as well as other temporary ones. In conjunction with the Castle Museum, York Art Gallery and York St Mary's, the museum is managed by the independent charitable trust Yorkshire Museum Trust.

The Yorkshire Museum's colonnaded entrance.

This life-size statue of Mars, the Roman god of war, was recovered from the local vicinity and is believed to be one of the finest Roman sculptures found in Britain.

Recovered locally in Stonegate is the carved marble head of the Roman Emperor Constantine, who was crowned Emperor while in York.

A model of a Norman soldier.

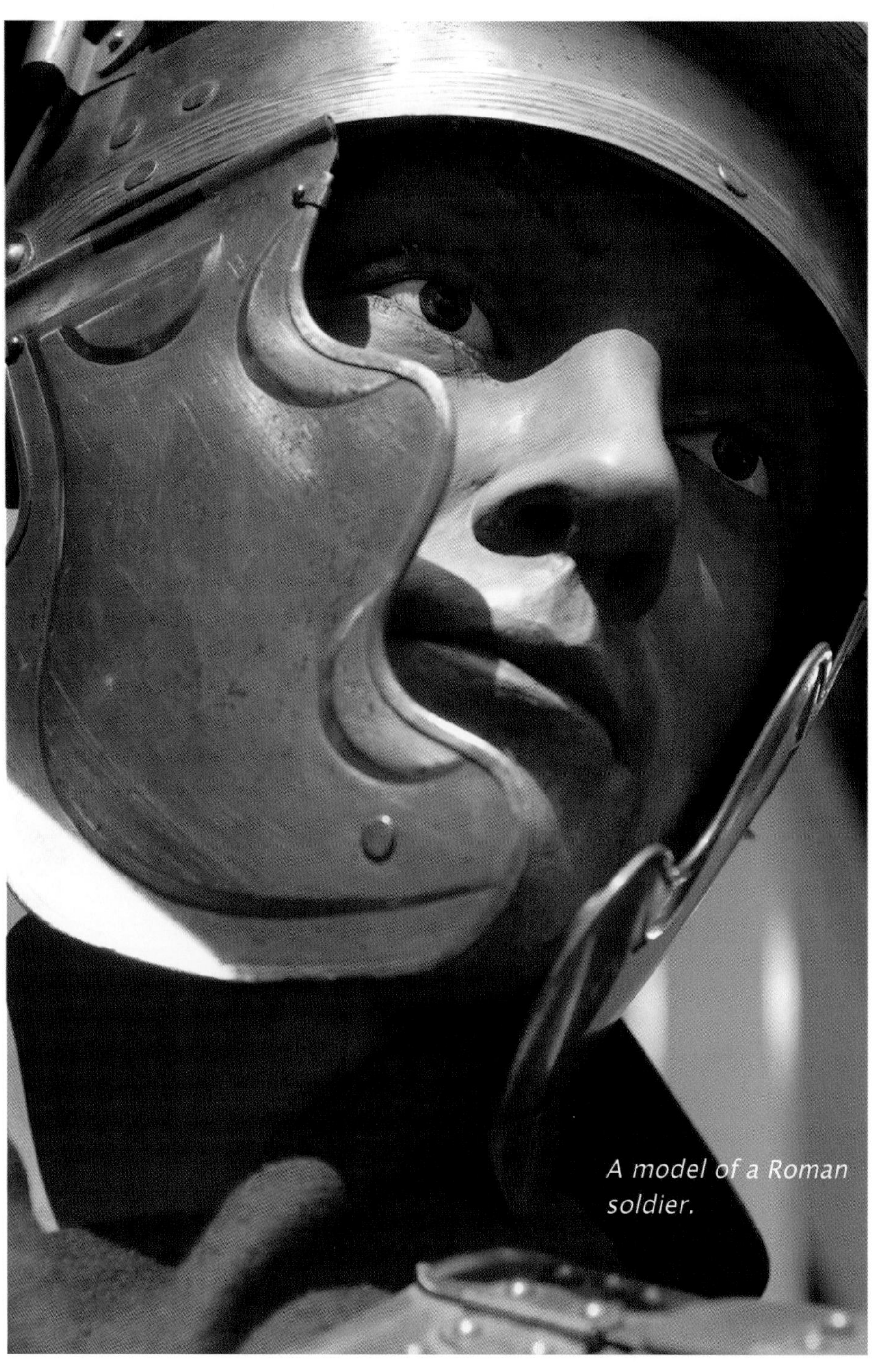

A model of a Roman soldier.

The history of the abbey and its inhabitants can be discovered in more detail among the ruins and foundations in the basement of the museum.

St Mary's Abbey vestibule, with the reconstructed chapter house entrance.

ST MARY'S ABBEY

Built in 1088 on the site of a previous monastery dedicated to St Olave, St Mary's Abbey was once one of the most powerful and wealthiest Benedictine monasteries in the country. The foundation stone of the abbey was reputedly laid by William the Conqueror's son. Some of the monks believed that the accumulated wealth of the monastery should be shared with the poor and that the regime of St Mary's Abbey should be stricter. This dispute led to a breakaway group of monks, led by Prior Richard, forming the Cistercian Fountains Abbey in Ripon. Under Henry VIII's Dissolution of the Monasteries in the 16th century, the abbey suffered the same fate as the other English-based monastic establishments and was disbanded, with its property and land being seized by the Crown. After its dissolution, the former abbey became a royal residence for use when the king visited York, but gradually it fell into disrepair and eventual ruin. The site was excavated by the Yorkshire Philosophical Society in the 1820s.

YORK OBSERVATORY

The oldest working observatory in Yorkshire, this octagonal building was constructed within the Museum Gardens in 1833. Housing a major part of the Yorkshire Museum astronomy collection, its telescope was used to calculate the exact time of day by the position of the stars and would then set the still surviving Barraud of London clock to the exact time - which is always four minutes and 20 seconds behind Greenwich Mean Time. During the mid-19th century the clock was considered to be the most accurate in the city and a charge would be levied for anyone wishing to set their own timepiece to that of the clock. Although not the original observatory telescope, the current early-19th-century, four-inch refractor telescope is still in operational use and was made locally by the distinguished York instrument maker Thomas Cooke. In addition to offering tours of the building and equipment on display, the observatory continually stages a programme of astronomy-related events throughout the year, to which visitors are most welcome.

HOSPITIUM

Located close to the River Ouse, this abbey outbuilding may have been used to accommodate and feed pilgrims. Completely restored and renovated in 2008 by the Yorkshire Museum Trust, the Hospitium is now a very popular wedding and conference venue. One of the oldest timber-framed buildings in York, the lower masonry section of the building is believed to date from 1310, while the upper timber-framed storey was constructed approximately 100 years later.

A dusk floodlit view of the Hospitium main entrance.

The 15th-century river gateway ruins attached to the Hospitium.

ST LEONARD'S HOSPITAL, CHAPEL AND UNDERCROFT

Once one of the largest hospitals in mediaeval England, the foundations of St Leonard's extended far beyond the vaulted undercroft and chapel ruins that can be seen today. Established by William the Conqueror's son, William Rufus, this 11th-century hospital's Augustine canons also catered for the spiritual and religious needs of the poor, orphaned, sick and infirm residents. It was these religious roots and monastic principles that led to its demise during Henry VIII's Reformation of the Church, and the building was surrendered to the Crown in 1540. The closure of St Leonard's would deny York's residents a hospital for nearly 200 years.

St Leonard's Hospital ruins and undercroft.

ST MARY'S LODGE

Situated at the Marygate entrance to the Museum Gardens is the Grade I listed 15th-century gatehouse St Mary's Lodge. The adjoining arch is believed to date from the 12th century and it is here that the poor would seek alms from the abbey monks. Since the demise of St Mary's Abbey, the gatehouse has been used as a court, public house, offices and the headquarters for the Yorkshire Museum Trust.

A dusk floodlit view of St Mary's Lodge and the 12th-century arch.

St Mary's Lodge from the Museum Garden grounds.

MULTANGULAR TOWER

The Multangular Tower is located within the Museum Gardens and further details and images of it can be found within the York City Walls chapter of this publication.

QUEEN MARGARET'S ARCH

Although not contained within the Museum Gardens, Queen Margaret's Arch was part of the original abbey wall. A plaque there states that the opening was in honour of Princess Margaret, who resided at the abbey for two days while travelling north to marry James IV of Scotland in July 1503. However, the doorway may have been constructed some six years earlier for use by Henry VII as a shortcut from St Mary's Abbey to York Minster.

ART GALLERY

Completed in 1879 to a classical design by the York architect Edward Taylor, York Art Gallery was a purpose-built venue designed to host York's second Yorkshire Fine Art and Industrial Exhibition. Initially the Yorkshire Fine Art and Industrial Institution, the gallery was originally much larger and was at one time a popular location for many social occasions and events such as boxing and cock fighting. Purchased by the Corporation in 1892 to become the City Art Gallery, it continued to host further art and industrial exhibitions. Although damaged by an incendiary bomb during World War Two, the building was reconstructed after the war ended.

Completed at the same time as the art gallery, Exhibition Square is overlooked by a statue of the York artist William Etty. On sunny days the gallery café places its tables and chairs in the square, which is an excellent spot to watch the world pass by while admiring the view of Bootham Bar, York Minster towers and the nearby King's Manor.

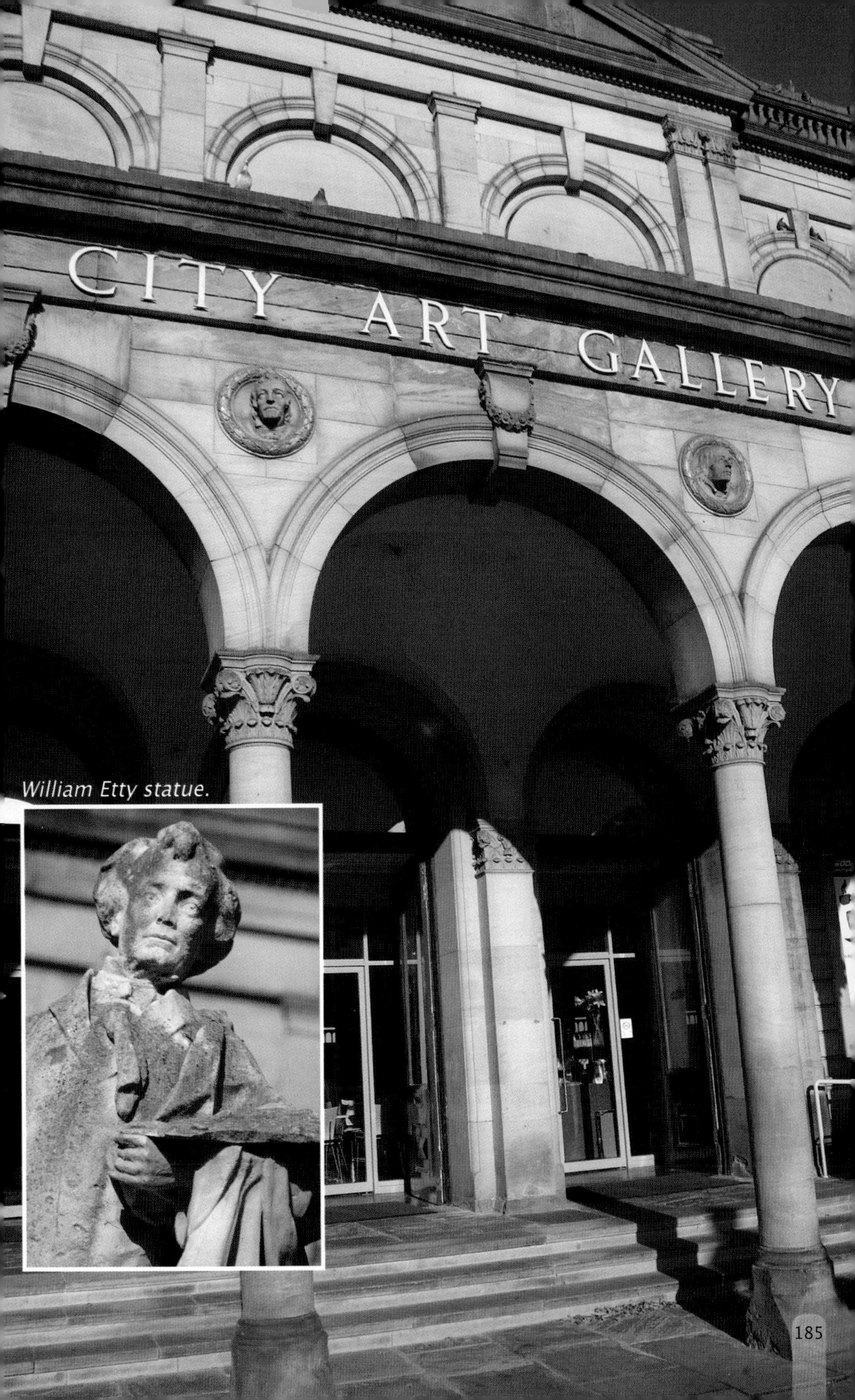

William Etty statue.

An evening view of York Art Gallery.

GALLERY

Collections are spread over two floors, with five areas displaying themed art and ceramic exhibitions. York Gallery's own collection of valuable and rare works of art and ceramics is further complemented by a programme of visiting temporary exhibitions and events.

York Art Gallery is managed by the Yorkshire Museum Trust, which at the time of writing offers free entry to the exhibitions.

Sacrifice

MANSION HOUSE

Reputed to be the first purpose-built civic residence in England, Mansion House stands elegant and assertive over the picturesque St Helen's Square. Some suggestions that the Palladian architectural style of Mansion House may be attributed to Lord Burlington are difficult to confirm. Another, perhaps more credible, theory is that there was a convergence of ideas from a committee of personnel who were nominated to oversee the building's completion. An initial allocated building budget of £1,000 was quickly spent and required several further refinancing requests. After five years, Mansion House was finally completed in 1730.

Running the full width of the house, the dining room provides an opulent setting for the Lord Mayor's official dinners. Elegantly furnished and tastefully decorated, the room contains many artefacts and treasures that are historically associated with the city.

St Helen's Square and Mansion House.

In 1668 Marmaduke Rawdon, a great benefactor to the city, bequeathed £100 to the city of York. He had left specific instructions that a 'drinking cup of pure gold' was to be purchased for use by the Lord Mayor. In addition, Marmaduke also bequeathed the sum of £10 for the purchase of a silver chamber pot, which apparently was an essential accessory for any grand social event of that period. The gold cup stands slightly askew, testifying to the softness and purity of the gold.

Detail of the Great Mace.

Elected for a period of 12 months, the Lord Mayor uses Mansion House both as an official home and as a place for entertaining and hosting visiting international and British dignitaries. Other than their duties as chairman of the City Council, the Lord Mayor of York's role tends to be primarily ceremonial. In a custom dating back centuries, the Sigismund Sword and Great Mace are carried in front of the Lord Mayor on civic occasions.

Made by a silversmith named Claudius Tirrell in 1647, the silver gilt Great Mace replaced an earlier smaller mace, which is no longer in existence.

THE SIGISMUND SWORD

Originally forged for Emperor Sigismund in 1416, the Sigismund Sword was eventually presented to the city in 1439. In an ancient custom visiting monarchs stop at Micklegate Bar to touch the State Sword before entering the city.

THE BOWES SWORD

Dating from 1549, the Bowes Sword was presented to the city by Sir Martin Bowes. Apparently the sword accompanied King James VI of Scotland to London, where he was to be crowned King James I of England in 1603. It is said that when the sword was returned to York, many of the jewels and gold trimmings were missing.

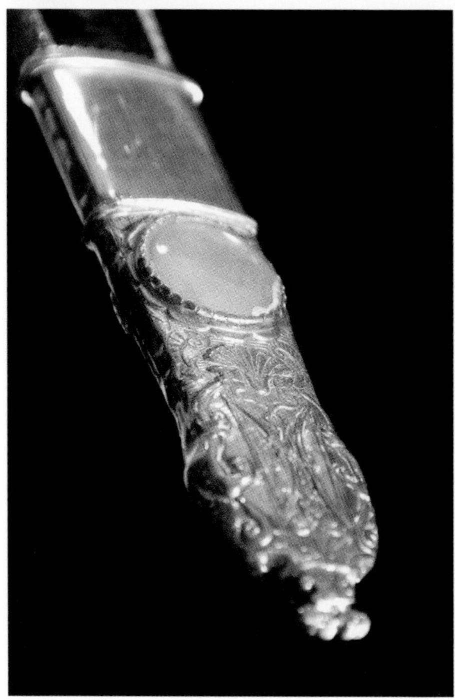

STATEROOM

It is easy to see why this magnificent stateroom has an impressive history of grand stately banquets and royal visitors. Sitting dominant above the fireplaces at each end of the room is the York and Royal coat of arms.

In 1999 a successful restoration project between York City Council and York Civic Trust worked hard to ensure that Mansion House was restored to its former glory. It is now available for private hire and is open to visitors at times specified by the City Council.

THE GUILDHALL

The site of the Guildhall's predecessor, the Commonhall, is believed to be in the same position as or in the near vicinity of the current structure. Sharing the cost for the building work between the Guild of St Christopher and the Corporation enabled the York Guild to keep their wine in the cellar and have periodic use of the interior rooms for stipulated annual festive periods. Also used as a Court of Justice, its City Assizes trials included that of Saint Margaret Clitherow.

Until its demolition in 1810, council meetings were normally conducted in a chamber room on Ouse Bridge. The relocation of the council meetings required extensions to the Guildhall in both the early and late 19th century.

Sandwiched between St Helen's Square and the River Ouse, access to York Guildhall is via the Mansion House Arch. However, the external aesthetic splendour of this magnificent 15th-century late mediaeval building is perhaps best appreciated from the embankment of the River Ouse – indeed, the view offered from the embankment is one of York's most recognised vistas.

York Guildhall's interior is as impressive as its exterior.

On 29 April 1942 York Guildhall received a direct hit from an incendiary bomb during the notorious World War Two Baedeker Raids. Despite the devastating destruction caused by the bombing raid, the outer shell of the building stubbornly survived. Remaining dilapidated for many years after the devastating air raid, a decision was finally taken in 1956 to restore both the external architecture and internal fabric of the building to its former glory. Restoration work began in 1958 and the Guildhall was reopened by the Queen Mother on 21 June 1960. York Guildhall continues to be used by York City Council and is home to the council chamber, committee rooms and headquarters for the Chief Executive's department.

The Victorian Council Chambers.

WEST WINDOW

Designed and painted by the York glass painter H.W. Harvey, this is believed to be the third version of the Guildhall West Window. The original 1684 window by Henry Gyles was replaced with a memorial window dedicated to Alderman Meek, which in turn was completely destroyed in the 1942 bombing. Scenes painted on this magnificent 1960 West Window represent specific periods and personalities relating to York's long history, including the figures of Constantine the Great, the York artist William Etty and King Edward III.

YORK RAILWAY

Until the arrival of the railway, York remained – in comparison to some of its Yorkshire neighbours – relatively unscathed by the Industrial Revolution. Some consider this fortunate and one of the principal reasons why the city has retained much of its historic charm. Just as the Romans had influenced York's ancient history, the railway forged the modern shape and future of the city and its inhabitants.

York's first railway station opened just outside the perimeter of the city wall in 1839. The station was soon relocated to a supposedly more passenger-convenient position, within the wall boundaries on Toft Green. This new location required the city wall to be breached with a new arch, and as the frequency of trains increased an adjacent arch was added in 1845.

The railway arches and York City Wall.

York's position as a centre to the rail network ensured that it soon outgrew the expansion capability of the available real-estate within the walls. Designed by the railway architect Thomas Prosser, the new station took three years to complete and was opened in 1877. Just a short distance from its former location within the wall boundaries, the new station was at the time the largest in the country. The station's importance to the railway distribution network made it a target for German Luftwaffe during World War Two and in April 1942 the station was bombed.

HUDSON AND LEEMAN

Nicknamed 'The Railway King', George Hudson was a former York draper who became the beneficiary of a large inheritance which he shrewdly invested in, and became chairman of, the York and North Midland Railway Company. Serving as York's Lord Mayor on three occasions, his railway investments saw substantial growth and financial return, making him an extremely wealthy and influential man. At the height of his power and wealth, Hudson was investigated for unethical business practices, which resulted in his bankruptcy and subsequent imprisonment in York's Debtors' Prison.

After his downfall, a street named George Hudson Street was renamed Railway Street. As a sign that Hudson is still very much credited with the early development of York's rail industry, the street was again renamed George Hudson Street in 1971, 100 years after his death.

George Leeman was a political adversary of George Hudson, and as a practising, York-based lawyer he was instrumental in the demise of his opponent. Also a former Lord Mayor of the city, Leeman championed the growth of the railway in York and was appointed chairman of various rail companies. Located near the railway arches is a statue in memory of his political contribution to the city and the railway.

George Leeman Statue.

LUTYENS MEMORIAL

In memory of over 2,000 North Eastern Railway workers who enlisted and died fighting in World War One, the company commissioned Sir Edwin Lutyens to design a fitting memorial. Lutyens was also responsible for the design of a number of other war memorials, including the Cenotaph in London. The memorial is located adjacent to the walls on the site of the former railway station sidings.

A rooftop view of the York City Wall, railway arches and Lutyens Memorial, with York railway station in the distant background.

Lutyens Memorial with York Minster in the background.

ROYAL YORK HOTEL

Adjacent to the station is the Royal York Hotel, which was originally named 'The Royal Station Hotel'. Intended to meet the demands of well-heeled travellers, this elegant hotel was completed in 1878; a year after the station was built. In the foreground is a small graveyard which was the burial ground for those who suffered during the cholera epidemic in 1832.

NORTH EASTERN RAILWAY HEADQUARTERS

Completed in 1906 to designs by William Bell and Horace Field, the former headquarters of the North Eastern Railway is said to be a mixture of architectural styles.

NATIONAL RAILWAY MUSEUM

Until 1948 and the nationalisation of the rail network, many private rail companies retained and displayed their own historic rail artefacts, and it was not until the opening of the National Railway Museum (NRM) in York in 1975 that the bulk of an ever-increasing national collection could be displayed in one primary, dedicated and purpose-built location. Although elements of the national collection are also on exhibition in other British locations, the National Railway Museum is the largest museum of its type in the world. The museum collection includes historic engines, carriages,

rolling stock, works of art, documents and photographic archives.

This award-winning museum, which attracts almost one million visitors every year, is a first-class, family orientated, must-see attraction, which at the time of writing offers free entry.

All three of the massive display halls are interlinked. The Great Hall, Works and Station Hall each offer themed exhibitions.

GREAT HALL

Located in a former engine shed, this immense exhibition features trains and rolling stock from past and present eras. Primarily of British manufacture, an impressive array of exhibits range from a sectioned replica of Stephenson's *Rocket* to the Eurostar, and even Japan's Bullet train.

MALLARD LOCOMOTIVE

On 3 July 1938 the world speed steam traction record was broken by the *Mallard* locomotive engine, which is now on display at the museum, as it reached a speed of 126 miles per hour (202.8 km per hour), making it the world's fastest steam engine.

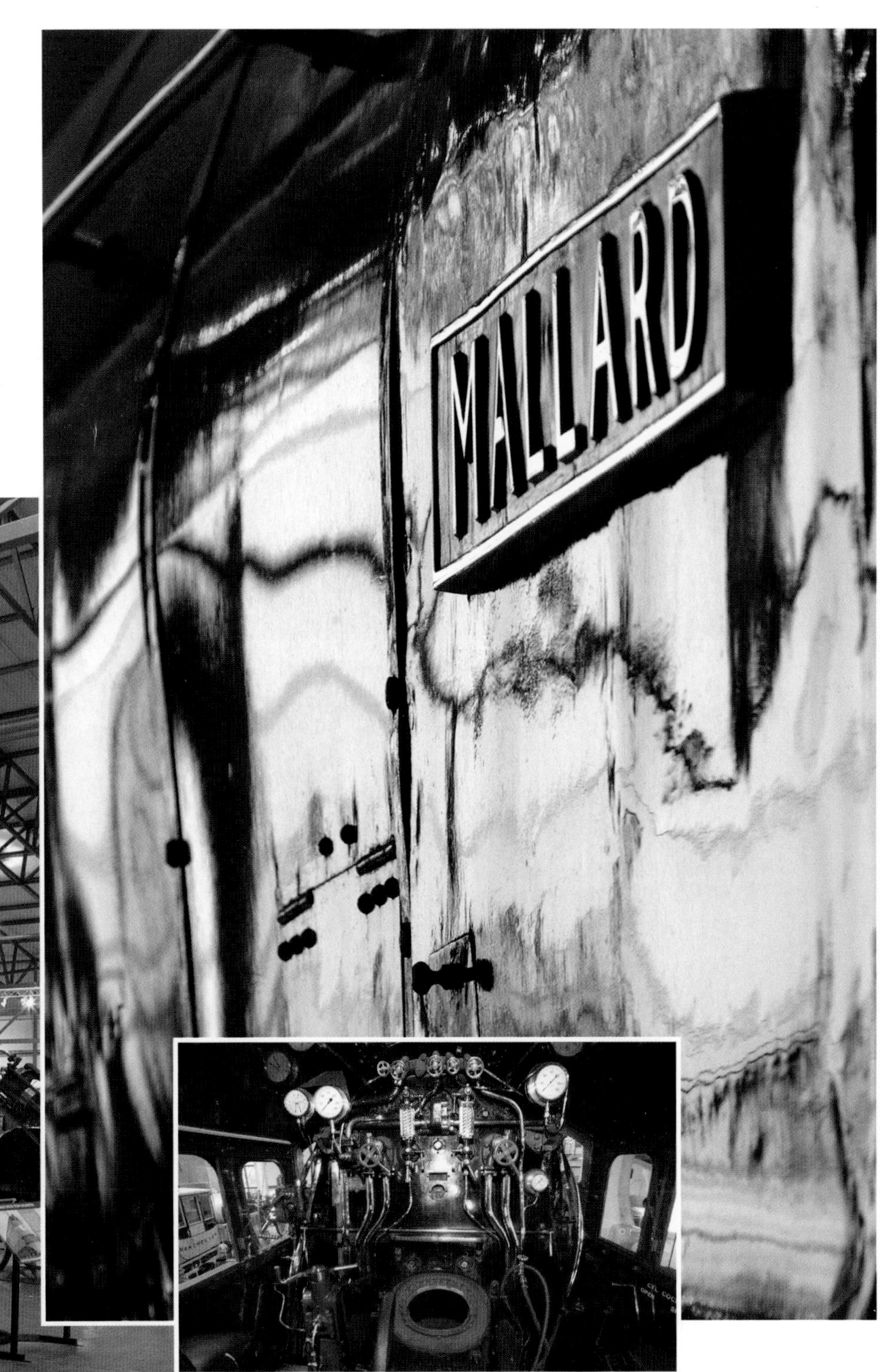
MALLARD

STEPHENSON'S *ROCKET* REPLICA

EUROSTAR

A section of the Euro Tunnel and Eurostar engine is on display in the Great Hall.

BULLET TRAIN

Capable of travelling at over 130 miles per hour, the Shinkansen Bullet Train is said to have revolutionised modern rail travel. Presented to the NRM by the West Japan Railway Company (JR-West), this is the only Bullet Train outside Japan. Transportation of the train from Japan to the NRM was said to be an engineering feat in its own right.

The locomotive turntable in the Great Hall.

HARDWICKE
790
52/363 BUILT BY 1954
JOHN BOYD & CO (ENGRS) LTD
ANNAN SCOTLAND
49

790
1293

THE WORKS

The NRM Works opened in 1999 within the former York Diesel Locomotive Depot and comprised of three additional exhibition areas, including the Workshop, Working Railway and the Warehouse.

THE WAREHOUSE

A replica of a large railway distribution store, the Warehouse contains over 750,000 individual objects. Exploration of the aisles will unveil a treasure chest of intriguing historic and modern rail travel items.

THE WORKSHOP

Real smells, sights and sounds of a steam-engine workshop are experienced during a stroll around the Workshop's elevated gallery, which offers NRM visitors a bird's eye perspective of skilled engineers working on current restoration and conservation projects.

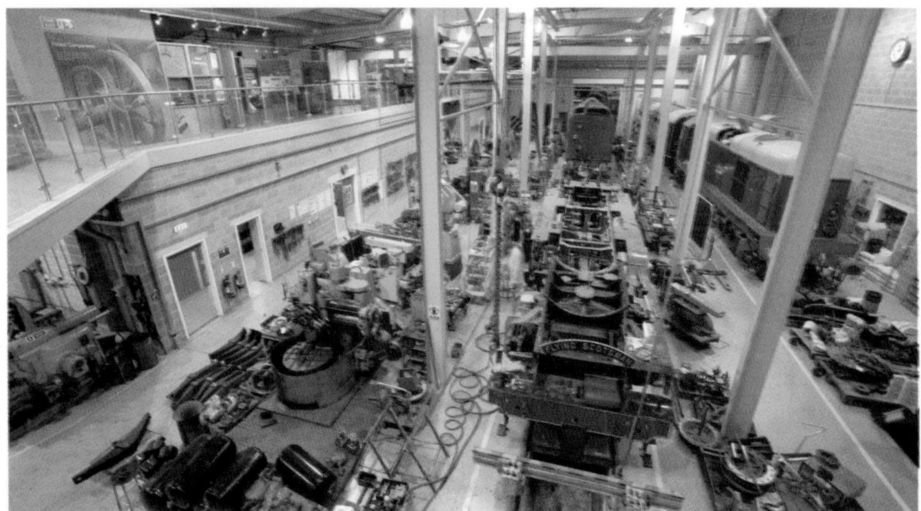

The Flying Scotsman *under major restoration in the Workshop.*

THE FLYING SCOTSMAN

Built in Doncaster at a cost of just under £8,000, the Sir Herbert Nigel Gresley-designed *Flying Scotsman* was introduced to service in 1924. Twice making history, in 1928 when she made the first non-stop long distance journey from London to Edinburgh in a time just exceeding eight hours, then again in 1934 she was recorded as the first steam traction train to reach the speed of 100 miles per hour, the history of *the Flying Scotsman* is both eventful and well documented. A national campaign to stop this iconic and much admired train from being sold outside the UK resulted in public and commercial financial donations to keep her in British hands. It was this successful campaign that delivered *the Flying Scotsman* into the hands of the National Railway Museum in 2004.

STATION HALL

Formerly the main freight station for York, Station Hall is now home to the NRM's prestigious Palace on Wheels exhibition. Displays include great works of art and the royal carriages that conveyed members of the Royal family – from Queen Victoria to Queen Elizabeth II – in luxurious style and comfort.

The Palace on Wheels exhibition.

Popular with visitors, especially the children, the NRM operates a Road Train taxi service between the city centre and the museum. The service operates on a frequent basis during peak tourist months.

RIVER OUSE

Formed from the River Ure at Cuddy Shaw Reach, north west of York, the River Ouse meanders past many historic Yorkshire towns, sites and areas of natural beauty before completing its 84km (52 mile) journey at Trent Falls on the River Trent. The river has, without doubt, substantially contributed to the city of York's rich heritage and commercial fortune. However, these good tidings have not been without remuneration and the city has experienced severe flooding for many centuries. Despite comprehensive flood defences – which are normally capable of coping with the river's unpredictable intensity and levels – bridges have been swept away and lives lost, but not for many years.

The River Ouse with St Mary's river tower and Scarborough Railway Bridge in the background.

Once a major inland port, the commercial warehouses and quays on York's waterfront have now been replaced by smart residential dwellings, modern offices, tempting cuisine and traditional public houses. The waterway and embankments are no longer burdened with the transit of raw products and commercial goods, but have found new vigour within the leisure and tourist industries.

A river sightseeing boat with the Guildhall and Lendal Bridge in the background.

Marygate Landing and St Mary's river tower.

Canada geese with St Mary's river tower in the background.

LENDAL BRIDGE

With the arrival of the new railway station at Tanner Row in the 19th century, pedestrian traffic wishing to cross the river increased dramatically. A ferry service that had operated between Barker and Lendal Tower for many centuries was now considered inadequate to cope with the demand and a new bridge was commissioned. Designed by William Dredge, the building of Lendal Bridge began in 1860, but less than a year into its construction it collapsed, killing five of the workmen. Thomas Page then assumed responsibility for the construction of the second version of the bridge, which

was finally completed in 1863 at a cost of approximately £35,500 – Page was also responsible for the design of York's Skeldergate Bridge and London's Westminster Bridge. Aesthetically pleasing, the parapet of this iron ornate bridge is adorned with various coats of arms and Victorian-style lighting.

Lendal Bridge and the toll house.

Lendal Bridge's ornate parapet and lamps.

A dusk view from Lendal Bridge.

Now being used as cafés, the small gatehouses at either end of the bridge were responsible for the collection of tolls, which were charged until they were abolished in 1894.

The River Ouse waterfront public houses and restaurants at the rear of Coney Street.

OUSE BRIDGE

Dating from the Roman era, a number of structures have been used to cross the river at or near the Ouse Bridge. One of the mediaeval predecessors supported residential dwellings, shops, a chapel and civic buildings at either end of the stone bridge, which collapsed into the river in 1564. The accident, caused by severe flooding and the collapse of the central arch, reportedly caused the death of 12 people. A picturesque replacement bridge was said to be one of the largest in Europe and a popular vista for artists and engravers, some of whom compared the 81ft single span bridge with that of Venice's Rialto Bridge. Completed in 1566, the predecessor to the present Ouse Bridge lasted until the early 19th century when it was demolished to make way for the Peter Atkinson-designed structure we see today. Completed in 1820, tolls for the new bridge were charged until 1829.

The public houses and restaurants at King's Staith make this a popular mooring for leisure craft and tourist boats.

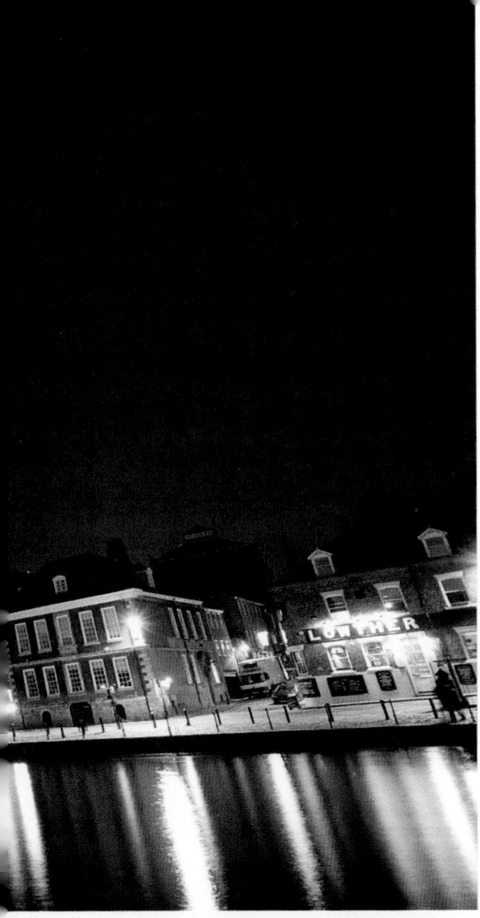
LOWTHER

KINGS ARMS
KING STREET
(FORMERLY KERGATE)

the
waterfront
Steak &
Seafood
Restaurant
en-suite rooms
available
t: 01904
671108

SKELDERGATE BRIDGE

Partially attributable to the railway and its ancillary industries, the population of York grew throughout the 19th century. The ferry crossing which operated at Skeldergate was considered inadequate to cope with increased commercial and tourist traffic. Designed by Thomas Page, who died before its construction, the Skeldergate Bridge took almost three years to complete and was fully opened in March 1881 – the completion

of the project was overseen by Thomas Page's son, George Page. Tolls were charged on the bridge until 1914. The toll house contained a bridge opening mechanism, which has now been removed, that allowed larger ships to transit slightly further upriver to the quays and unload their cargo. Like Lendal Bridge, also designed by Thomas Page, the iron bridge's parapet is ornate and Gothic in appearance.

Looking upriver towards Ouse Bridge from Skeldergate Bridge.

Views from Terry Avenue en route to the Millennium Bridge.

Looking down the river from Skeldergate Bridge.

A stroll along the aesthetic inner-city riverbank will rapidly transport you from historic buildings and structures to scenic rural pathways.

MILLENNIUM BRIDGE

Constructed at a cost of over £4 million, York Millennium Bridge was officially opened in 2001. The steel pedestrian and cycle bridge design is said to have been inspired by the spokes of a bicycle wheel.

WAR MEMORIAL GARDENS

Opened in 1925, the Leeman Road War Memorial Garden is York's principal Garden of Remembrance and hosts the annual Remembrance Service in November. Located just outside the city wall perimeter and adjacent to the River Ouse, this small, pretty garden offers peaceful seclusion from the busy surroundings.

Glasgow

London

Cardiff

Alistair and Jan Campbell are the founders and principal photographers of UK City Images. This elite and independent image library specialises in providing the travel and media industries with high-quality photographs of UK city scenes and landmarks.

Portraying the richness and diversity of UK city architecture helps promote Britain as a desirable tourist destination, to both a global and British audience. Images are captured in a style that is deliberately designed to excite positive interest in their location and history.

All images within this publication are the sole copyright of UK City Images, who are pleased to offer a facility to purchase either print or data copies to both commercial and private customers. Sales enquiries should be directed to sales@ukcityimages.com.

An exciting array of other UK city scenes and landmarks, plus additional York images, can be viewed from their website at **www.ukcityimages.com.**

Liverpool

Birmingham

Newcastle

Portsmouth